The Land of the Living

David Lan was born in Cape Town where he trained as an actor. He has lived in London since 1972. His plays, adaptations and libretti have been produced by the National Theatre, the Royal Court, the RSC, the Almeida and Aldborough. He has published an ethnography, *Guns and Rain: Guerrillas and Spirit Mediums in Zimbabwe*, and a memoir *As if by Chance: journeys, theatres, lives*. He was writer-in-residence at the Royal Court, artistic director/CEO of the Young Vic, consulting artistic director to the PAC/NY and theatre associate at BAM. He is co-producer of the global journeys of *Little Amal* in support of refugees, as well as of *The Herds*, a journey from the Congo Basin to the Arctic Circle by life-size puppet animals fleeing the climate crisis.

DAVID LAN

The Land of the Living

faber

First published in 2025
by Faber and Faber Limited
The Bindery, 51 Hatton Garden
London, EC1N 8HN

Typeset by Brighton Gray
Printed and bound in the UK by CPI Group (Ltd), Croydon CR0 4YY

All rights reserved
© David Lan, 2025

David Lan is hereby identified as author
of this work in accordance with Section 77 of the
Copyright, Designs and Patents Act 1988

All rights whatsoever in this work, amateur or professional,
are strictly reserved. Applications for permission for any use
whatsoever including performance rights must be made in
advance, prior to any such proposed use, to
Judy Daish, United Agents Limited,
12–26 Lexington Street, London W1F 0LE

No performance may be given unless a licence
has first been obtained

A CIP record for this book
is available from the British Library

ISBN 978-0-571-39376-3

Printed and bound in the UK on FSC® certified paper in line with our continuing
commitment to ethical business practices, sustainability and the environment.
For further information see faber.co.uk/environmental-policy

Our authorised representative in the EU for product safety is
Easy Access System Europe, Mustamäe tee 50, 10621 Tallinn, Estonia
gpsr.requests@easproject.com

The Land of the Living was first performed in the
Dorfman auditorium of the National Theatre, London,
on 9 September 2025, with the following cast:

Mayor Atilla Akinci
Dora Kate Duchêne
George Michael Fox
Pawel Hubert Hanowicz
Elise Caroline Loncq
Olga Avital Lvova
Bill Michael Marcus
Theresa Anastasia Martin
Thomas's Father Marek Oravec
Thomas's Mother Cosima Shaw
Ruth Juliet Stevenson
Anna Sasha Syzonenko
Thomas Tom Wlaschiha
Young Thomas Darcy Tosun, Anton Vehring, Artie Wilkinson-Hunt

All other roles played by members of the company

Director Stephen Daldry
Set Designer Miriam Buether
Costume Designer Nicky Gillibrand
Lighting Designer James Farncombe
Sound Designer Gareth Fry
Composer Paul Englishby
Movement Director Paul McGill
Fight and Intimacy Director Maisie Carter
Casting Naomi Downham
Language and Dialect Coach Victoria Woodward
Voice Coach Cathleen McCarron
Associate Director Jane Moriarty
Staff Director Júlia Levai

In memory of Gitta Sereny

Thanks to the NT Studio and all the actors who most generously took part in workshops.

Atilla Akinci, Rhys Bailey, Debbie Chazen, Kate Duchêne, Michael Fox, Hubert Hanowicz, Akiya Henry, Alex Jarrett, Tim Jupiter, Joseph Kloska, Caroline Loncq, Avital Lvova, Jo McInnes, Michael Marcus, Anastasia Martin, Ewan Miller, Justine Mitchell, Hattie Morahan, Marek Oravec, Cosima Shaw, Lex Shrapnel, Benjamin Spalding, Juliet Stevenson, Sasha Syzonenko, Darcy Tosun, Ami Tredrea, Anton Vehring, Mark Washcke, Ben Whishaw, Artie Wilkinson-Hunt, Tom Wlaschiha.

Characters

Ruth
late sixties and early twenties

Thomas
mid-fifties

Dora
forties, Ruth's deputy

Theresa
twenties, Ruth's assistant

Olga
a Soviet liaison officer

George
an American army officer

Young Thomas
ten

Thomas's Father

Thomas's Mother

Elise
fifty, Ruth's mother

Bill
late twenties, an American army photographer

Anna
a Ukrainian mother

Gertrude
a German mother

Mr and Mrs Brandauer

Pawel, Ewa and Małgorzata

Marguerite
a maid

German Priest, Polish Priest, Cook,
German Countess and Guests, German Doctor, Optician

German Mayor, Polish Mayor

Children, Carers, Translators, Researchers,
Soldiers, Officers

Germans, Russians, Ukrainians, Americans, Poles

THE LAND OF THE LIVING

The main location is Ruth's flat in London in 1990.
All other locations are within her memory of events in 1945
in southern Germany, Alsace and central Poland.
All memory scenes take place chronologically.

From time to time children appear, but only Young Thomas
is seen. The presence of the others is evoked by their voices
as well as the words and actions of the onstage characters.

Languages spoken, apart from English, are German,
Bavarian, Ukrainian, Polish and Russian.

All characters are invented,
the historical circumstances are real.

Act One

RUTH'S FLAT IN LONDON 1990

Thomas But before you say anything . . .

Ruth *I've* not said a word.

Thomas (*angry*) I want to be clear, I'm not at all angry.

Ruth Oh. Well, nor am I with you, though you were abominably late. Not that I was at a loose end. The life of a hack, ruled by magazine deadlines. (*Laughs.*) Did I say ruled or ruined? Overshadowed.

Thomas I'm expected the old place – out of the underground, turn right, turn left . . .

Ruth My dear, *no one* can find this building. How they arrange the street numbers, letters, *books* wind up in entirely the wrong hands. To sort it out I invite my neighbours, 'take potluck', Bill does his outlandish cooking, I play Mum which I adore . . .

   Thomas laughs.

What triggered this desperate mood? Did you think you'd lost me?

Thomas The truth is, I found you quite easily. I sat for an hour by the lake in the park –

Ruth In this heat? Excuse me, when did you arrive in London? You didn't come straight from the airport . . . ? So, when you phoned me, you were . . . ?

Thomas In Brooklyn.

Ruth But won't you lie down, even for a moment, there's the room the children use, perhaps you'd prefer mine . . . ?

Don't hide your beautiful face – and sit. Something to eat? Don't say no. Some tea.

She starts to make tea.

Our little street's a dead end though 'spiritually' (*laughs*) we're bohemian, downstairs *two* poets and a painter, not *too* Picasso cliché, and, of course, Bill. We put his photographs up again the moment we moved in. 1940s, 1950s, the sixties, all sadly golden years for war photography. On his sixtieth birthday he gave you 'Battle of Kapyong', am I wrong? Korea but not too blood and guts. My dear, the question you asked takes me back to the dawn of time so I'm checking, is my memory in working order?

Thomas It was 'Battle of Kapyong', it hangs in my apartment.

Ruth Bill's in Vienna shooting cityscapes for my feature for *Vogue*, European edition.

Thomas Will you answer my question?

Ruth Well, that's a separate question. Sit down. All my life, all *your* life, I've struggled with this – was what I did 'wrong'?

She is struggling.

Thomas Shall I get you some water?

He scans the room.

Ruth Am I so boring? What are you looking for?

Thomas The piano.

Ruth There, you laid your splendid hat on it as you came in.

Thomas The Bösendorfer!

Ruth Oh, if we'd made room for that old girl there'd be no space for Bill or for me.

Thomas But I'd have taken it.

Ruth To New York?

Thomas At any price.

Ruth I didn't think, forgive me, in the confusions of moving . . .

Thomas What's this?

He plays a few notes on an old upright piano.

Ruth *Never never change* – pom
It's for Bill to play his pom pom.
Keep that dee dee dee – pom
Can't you please arrange it?
'Cause I . . .

Thomas sits and plays the opening bars of the Piano Quintet in G by Shostakovich.

Don't rush me. It's a dark wood, I have to find my way. The war . . . *My* war was in Washington, State Department, editing protocols for a new world. Ceasefire! 'Fly out to Germany,' become a cog in the UN machine. There were four zones, British, French, the Soviets' and mine – Bavaria, the American zone. The devastation! Imagine, city squares levelled by our English bombs, baroque facades, high tenements for German workers – boom . . . All over the country labour camps, the death camps in Poland, Ukraine – the Allies flung open the gates, the streets of Europe flooded with 'DPs', displaced people, it was as if the earth could hold no more and they had welled up out of the ground.

A COURTYARD IN THE CITY OF PASSAU IN BAVARIA
1945

Dora and Theresa are in UNRRA uniform.
Ruth is in charge. Dora, the oldest, is Ruth's deputy.
Theresa, the youngest, is Ruth's assistant.

Dora (*to Theresa*) These little ones have built a shelter out of hubcaps and cardboard.

Theresa (*to Dora*) So inventive.

Dora (*to Theresa*) Desperate, I think is the word you're looking for.

Ruth (*to Thomas*) Dashing into the dark after a truck loaded with medicines . . . In fact, it was Yannik our heart-throb driver with his marvellous long hair, rare in those days, who was heading in the *right* direction whereas I (*laughs*), 'wrong-headed Ruth' . . . My foot into a pothole, ooh la la, for a month I dared not put any weight . . . My point – it was chance.

Thomas What was?

Ruth That I was grounded not ten miles from your village . . . As the armies, mile by mile, liberated towns, our job was to care for the liberated human beings, feed them, find them shelter from the rain, whatever they needed. My brief was tightly defined – help sisters find their brothers, husbands their long-lost wives but, above all, help them to get home. But around every corner were children – I might say hordes but that's dehumanising.

Children *Zostaw ich! Odejdź! Chodź z nami!* [Leave them! Get away! Come with us!]

Dora (*to Ruth*) Those two little ones were hiding in a pit. (*Of Theresa.*) She fell in, sprained her poor knee.

Theresa (*to Dora*) Forget it, it's nothing.

Olga (*a Soviet liaison officer*) Yes, I am Doctor Polunina, hello, liaison officer responsible for wellbeing of all Soviet citizens.

George (*to Olga*) Not in the American zone!

Olga We are aware many of our children have been removed into US facility, contrary to globally agreed protocol!

Ruth (*to Olga*) Whose protocol is this? (*To George.*) Surely the US doesn't care which country these poor creatures were born in?

George We don't, we'd take 'em all.

Ruth (*to George*) Good for you.

George But so many, our outfit hasn't capacity, not nearly.

Olga I am ten years paediatrician, these come with me. (*To children.*) What are you? *Russki?* Yes? No? I think so.

Olga and the Russian children have gone.

Thomas (*to Ruth*) Which children were these?

Ruth (*to Thomas*) They'd come from the east, all over the conquered territories, forced to work – 'work', my God – in steel mills, munitions, with their sharp eyes and agile little fingers. Unshackled, emaciated, pitted with scars.

Ruth (*to Dora*) And this little girl, why is she lying on the ground?

Dora (*to Ruth*) She's not on the ground, give your colleagues *some* credit.

Ruth (*to Dora*) Her blanket's streaked with excrement.

George has gone.

(*To Thomas.*) The Allies herded them into camps. Many refused, formed gangs, thieving out of need, causing chaos for the Germans who they loathed but also for us Allies – who *could* they trust after their experience?

Thomas But that wasn't me.

Ruth I want to remind you how widespread was the misery, the disorder which was, forgive me, outside your experience.

Thomas No, I was one of the happy ones.

Ruth (*to Dora and Theresa*) So, what do we do?

Dora About what?

Ruth (*to Thomas*) Children were not my business. I was a child myself. I was twenty. And then . . .

A FARMYARD 1945

Theresa Ruth!

Anna is a poorly dressed DP.

We found her in the stables.

Ruth She was *living* there?

Theresa Hiding under straw. Anna, come, we'll find you warm clothing.

Dora Tell Ruth what happened.

Theresa She has two children, her girl five, her boy seven. Both were taken.

Dora But not to work, not at that age?

Ruth Anna, darling, who took your children?

Theresa *Khto zabrav vechykh ditey?*

Anna *Ne znayu.*

Translator She doesn't know.

Ruth When was this?

Theresa She said three years ago she left them in the playground for twenty minutes.

Dora How could they survive, so little?

Ruth (*to Anna*) I'm Ruth, born Alsace which is sometimes France, sometimes Germany, it's bewildering. You're from?

Theresa (*simultaneous*) *Ya Rut, narodylasya v El'zasi, yakyy chasom frantsuz'kyy, a inodi nimets'kyy, tse chudovo. Zvidky vy?*

Anna *Ya z Lucka.*

Translator She's from Lutsk.

Ruth Which is?

Theresa Ukraine. Poland. Poland-Ukraine.

Anna *Ya na nashomu rynku prodayu kachok.*

Translator In the market she sells ducks.

Ruth What kind – mallards, pintails?

Translator *Yaki kachky, kryzhni, shylokhvosty?*

Anna *Zhyri, dlya smazhennya.*

Translator Fat, for roasting.

Ruth Has she any idea where her children were taken?

Translator *Vy znayete, kudy povezly ditey?*

Anna *My chuly Passau.*

Ruth (*astonished*) Passau?

Theresa Passau.

Translator Passau.

Ruth But that's not so far down the road. Her children were brought to Passau?

Theresa It's a rumour, in fact she knows nothing.

Anna *Vden' kachok pasu, vnochi ditey shukayu.*

Translator (*simultaneous*) By day she feeds ducks, at night she searches for her children.

Anna (*to Ruth*) *Miy syn Orest, vin duzhe rozumnyy. U n'oho svitle volossya i velyka rodymka na shchotsi. Moyiy don'tsi Solomiyi bulo dva roky, koly yiyi zabraly. U neyi shram na likti. Chy mozhete vy yikh znayty?* [My son Orest is smart, he has fair hair and a birthmark on his cheek. My daughter Solomiya was two when they took her, she has a scar on her elbow. Can you find them?]

As Anna speaks, more children arrive . . .

Children *Chcemy wyjść! Jesteśmy głodni! Chcemy uciec!* [We want out! We're hungry! We want to get away!]

Ruth (*to Dora*) Could hers be amongst ours?

Dora What did she say? *Our* children? Which are they?

THE COURTYARD IN PASSAU 1945

Ruth (*to Thomas*) Did I want it?

Children *Jesteśmy głodni! Chcemy czekolady! Czekolada, chcemy jej!* [We're hungry! We want chocolate! Chocolate, we want it!]

Ruth (*to Thomas*) There was need, I had an impulse, I acted on it.

Thomas (*to Ruth*) But what did you know of child psychology?

Ruth (*laughing*) Or any aspect of child management. Even so, all at once –

Dora (*to Theresa*) Why her?

Ruth (*to Thomas*) I found myself in charge –

Dora (*to Theresa*) I'm twice her age.

Ruth (*to Thomas*) – of an enormous unit for children.

Children *Papierosy! Chcemy papierosów!* [Cigarettes, we want cigarettes!]

Theresa (*to Dora*) But where will they sleep?

Dora (*to Theresa*) Never a moment to consider pros and cons.

Ruth (*to Thomas*) We were allocated a huge barn.

A BARN NEAR PASSAU 1945

Dora (*to Ruth*) It's not nearly big enough.

Children *Orangen! Orangen!* [Oranges! Oranges!]

Theresa (*to Ruth*) There's no glass in any of the windows.

Dora What are the high-ups playing at?

Ruth (*to the children*) What fruit I had I've given. Don't pretend to cry, you're a rotten actor.

Thomas (*to Ruth*) But those children were not part of 'the programme'.

Ruth (*to Thomas*) Then we didn't know there *was* a programme! Stay with me. The children I was in charge of knew exactly who they were and where they came from. We made notes of whatever they could tell us, sent it to the Central Tracing Bureau in Frankfurt where they searched for any surviving relatives.

Children *Äpfel! Äpfel!* [Apples! Apples!]

Ruth (*to the children*) Keep your eye out for GIs, they have crates full of apples, delicious.

American Soldier Kids are not allowed to goof around.

Theresa No, they're *our* children, *we're* responsible.

American Soldier (*to the children*) Move!

Dora Kindly not to bully!

Theresa Show respect, they do whatever Ruth asks them.

Ruth (*to Thomas*) If we bought all we needed in village stores, prices would skyrocket, so we swooped on villages, requisitioned mattresses, soap, light bulbs . . .

Dora (*of the American soldier*) Has he gone? (*To children.*) Off the truck, jokers, no one's going on a joyride. Boys, try to be useful, put those boxes on the trolley. Poor you, exhausted from doing nothing . . .

Child *Ale toalety sa pełne! Nie mam gdzie srać!* [But the toilets are full! I have nowhere to shit.]

Ruth Sorry, one shower block, that's it.

Children *Chodźmy! Chodźmy!* [Let's go, let's go!]

Ruth Dora! Rules! 'Not outside the fence unless with a military escort.'

Dora I've said it umpteen times, I'm Salvation Army, to me one army's like another as a bean to a bean. (*To children.*) Ignore her, she's worse than H—, worse than H—

Thomas (*laughing*) You, worse than Hitler?

Dora Than H—, H—, Harry Truman! Ha!

A BALLROOM IN THE SCHLOSS 1945

A big band plays, American male and female soldiers dance.

Ruth (*to George, shouting over the music*) But the children *need* supplies. Without a truck . . .

George Honey, I lend you transport, you give it to the UN. 'More.' *Nein*, even for you. Do you always wear your hair like so or is it special for wartime?

Ruth I have cows, I have horses, what I need is a field. If children plant seeds they're imagining a future.

George You want me to order farmers off their land?

Ruth If *you* can't, I'll find someone who can.

George Not through that door! We have clearance only for this wing of this whore's basilica!

Ruth goes through a door.

PRIVATE ROOMS OF THE SCHLOSS 1945

A dinner party – the Countess and her guests.

Countess Warm wishes to our friends the US Army . . .

Ruth (*of George*) Lieutenant Ridgeton is US Army.

Countess Oh, George and I . . .

Ruth *I* am UN Relief and Rehabilitation.

Countess *and* **Guests** (*toasting*) US Army!

Ruth (*to Thomas*) Of course, they were utterly bewildered to discover what, under their noses, had been going on.

A guest smashes a glass.

Countess Friedrich . . .

Guest 1 Why wait for them to smash everything?

Countess What is left is ours.

Guest 2 There'll be nothing left, nothing to come back to!

Ruth (*to Thomas*) Our marvellous barn – so many little feet, the floor very quickly was mud, we had water only two hours a day and the roof was falling in.

THE SCHLOSS – NEXT DAY 1945

Ruth (*to the Countess*) Your – what is this place?

Countess Schloss Moos, my castle. What of it?

Theresa (*high on a staircase*) There are forty-three rooms!

Countess I granted to US Army one half!

Ruth Such high airy spaces!

Dora Bales of blankets in the corridors!

Theresa Children, in! But wipe your feet!

Countess You cannot take all!

Child *Muszę zostać z Vanya, on jest moim bratem.* [I have to stay with Vanya, he's my brother.]

Theresa Your new brother, not your real brother.

Child *Z Vanya muszę być z nim zawsze.* [With Vanya, I must stay with him always.]

Countess My workers have lived here since 1750, you cannot throw them out with the rubbish!

Ruth Nonsense, they have family in the villages.

Theresa *Barrels* of pickled salmon! *Mountains* of salt beef!

Dora Bathrooms on every landing!

Countess I have breweries!

Child *Chłopcy, trzymajcie się swoich jaja, goraca woda!* [Boys, hold on to your balls, hot water!]

George Where's the bleeding-heart brigade?

Countess I have five hundred beehives!

Dora Anyone at all ill, find a corner out of the draught on this floor.

Children *Gdzie jest alkohol, panie? Gdzie sa butelki z alkoholem?* [Where's the booze, ladies? Where's the bottles of booze?]

Theresa You and you, upstairs. Watch your feet, marble is slippery.

George (*to Ruth*) We've found something I'd like you to see.

Ruth Something good?

American Soldier Not so good.

A SMALL ROOM IN THE SCHLOSS 1945

American soldiers are examining metal instruments.

George We're clearing out offices.

Ruth Dora! Theresa!

George Go ahead, ladies, take a look. These were locked neatly in specially made crates.

Ruth (*to George*) What are they for? (*To Dora and Theresa.*) Who has a suggestion?

Dora Perhaps some sort of carpentry?

Theresa If you force them, look, they slide up and down.

American soldiers bring in the German Doctor.

American Soldier 1 (*to George*) Lieutenant.

Ruth (*of the German Doctor, to George*) Who is he? What's he so frightened about? Oh. Has he been tortured?

George Absolutely not.

German Doctor (*terrified*) All the children came from the east.

Ruth Which children?

American Soldier 1 (*to the German Doctor*) If you lie again, I'll rip your head off.

Theresa (*of the German Doctor*) Watch out! He's pissing himself.

Ruth Open a window, let out the stink.

American Soldier 2 (*to the German Doctor*) Spell it out, from where in the east?

German Doctor Centuries ago, their families were exiled from these parts, they are all German orphans . . .

Thomas (*to Ruth*) He said the children were German?

German Doctor Lady, sir, I am highly trained surgeon, by specialised measuring it's easy to know which child is pure blood.

Theresa 'Pure blood'?

Dora Oh, my Lord Jesus. (*Of the instruments.*) These are for measuring children.

Theresa I don't understand. (*To the German Doctor.*) What can you learn about the blood of children by measuring them?

German Doctor Excuse me, *I* can't answer, I am only Doctor Schmelling, Professor Doctor Osvald Schmelling . . .

RUTH'S FLAT 1990

Thomas (*to Ruth*) But you must have known about this.

Ruth Of this we knew nothing. What urgently concerned us . . . Every country was claiming their children. To us each child was precious, we talked to them, one to one, their experience, their suffering. Our responsibility was get them home, *to their own families* if they'd survived but, at very least, to their own soil, their own rivers, their own mountains. We were terrified the Russian liaison officers would load them on trucks, as soon as they'd crossed the border, dump them. Worse, to Stalin any Russian who'd survived a German camp must be a traitor – bang bang!

Thomas Not children.

Ruth How could we be certain? So, we gave them the choice – go with your liaison officer or stay, take the chance that, through the Tracing Bureau, your mother, your father will find you.

Thomas The *children* had to choose?

Ruth With your feet up in a comfortable room, blinds keeping out the sun, it seems ridiculous, irresponsible even, but these young people had lived, some of them for years, under iron discipline. For once, let *them* make the decisions about their lives. Wait! We weren't fools. We struck a deal. We laid on classes – science, life drawing. Attend, take part in ball games, we'll allow no one, no one at all, to try to influence them as to what they should do.

Woman's Voice (*far away*) They're here!

THE SCHLOSS 1945

Ruth (*to Thomas*) The schloss, two nights after we'd settled in . . .

Russian soldiers sing.

Woman's Voice (*closer*) They're here!

Ruth Russian soldiers wearing uniforms we'd never seen park trucks across the street. We hurry out, chain the gate. (*To Olga.*) Here there are no children.

Olga That we do not believe. (*To a Russian soldier.*) *Ona izhet*. [She's lying.]

Thomas (*to Ruth*) You'd been tipped off?

Ruth (*laughing, to Thomas*) Of course, we'd hidden them deep in the forest. We allowed in liaison officers, no military, led them down corridors – empty room, empty room, empty, empty. As the trucks pulled away the children thronged back whooping, cheering our famous victory.

Sounds of triumphant children . . .

RUTH'S FLAT 1990

Ruth You don't fancy tea. Perhaps something stronger? You don't want to freshen up? Up to you.

She goes out.

THOMAS'S MOTHER'S HOUSE 1945

Young Thomas, aged ten, plays with a football while his Father cleans a rifle.

Thomas's Father *Die hast do du ghåd – wo håst as n lossn?* [You had them, where did you leave them?]

Young Thomas *I ho s ninads lossn.* [I didn't leave them anywhere.]

Thomas's Father *Dua net streitn. Du håst s ghåd, du muast s finna.* [Don't argue. You had them, you find them.]

Young Thomas *Do hånis jo.* [Found them!]

Thomas's Father *Basst, schick di, s is nua mea a hoibe Stunde dåg.* [Hurry, there's only half an hour of daylight left.]

Thomas's Mother *Na dammal du blaipst do.* [Thomas, you're staying.]

Young Thomas *I ho an Våttan sei Håntschua funna und iatzad muas I zon jong.* [I found Father's gloves, now I have to go hunting.]

Thomas's Mother *Mia zwoa mochma wos schäs, du und i.* [We'll do something nice, you and me.]

Young Thomas *Ui – eppa Blatzal båcha?* [Can we bake biscuits?]

Thomas's Mother *Jo, und du kosd ma vualesn. Ge her mei Schatzerl.* [Yes, and you can read to me. Come, my darling.]
  (*Singing.*)
  Schlaf, Kindlein, schlaf
  Der Vater hüt die Schaaf
  Die Mutter schüttelts Bäumelein
  Da fällt herab ein Träumelein
  Schlaf, Kindlein, schlaf . . .

RUTH'S FLAT 1990

Thomas is picking out the tune on the piano and singing to himself. Ruth comes in with a bottle of cognac and glasses. She listens to him.

Ruth You're right, this place is poky, you're used to far better, so are we, what can I do? My books don't sell as they did. For me it's early but for you it's – what? – mid-afternoon? No, I have it back to front, it's eight in the morning. So, we're in our own personal time zone.

She pours for him, then for herself. They drink.

So, we come to you.

Act Two

THE COURTYARD OF THE SCHLOSS 1945

A woman DP approaches Ruth singing a lament.

Ruth Her face, like the carving of a saint . . . (*To a Translator.*) What is that – Polish, Ukrainian . . . ?

The Translator speaks to the woman DP. She replies.

Translator (*to Ruth*) She wants to know will there be trains?

Ruth (*to the woman DP*) There will, my dear, more than enough but as to when . . .

The woman DP holds out an icon to Ruth.

Your poor, wasted arms. No, of course I can't accept this.

The woman DP prostrates herself.

Ridiculous, get up, my dear! Get up!

Translator (*to the woman DP*) Matulo, wstawajcie! [Mum, get up!]

The woman DP gets up and speaks quietly to Ruth. The Translator listens. The woman DP forces the icon into her hands.

Ruth (*to the Translator*) Tell me what she is saying, exactly.

Translator In some villages there can be found children from other places.

Ruth But 'places' means cities?

Translator Not at all.

Ruth Countries?

Translator It's a general statement. It refers to children who seem to have roots here but have, in fact, none.

Ruth Do you mean like our children from the factories?

Translator No, this has nothing to do with those who were brought here openly as workers.

Ruth Then who are they?

Translator I could say she speaks of some kind of '*special* children', *specjalne dzieci*.

Ruth (*to Thomas*) Europe was a maze, one lived like a spy picking up clues.

Thomas (*to Ruth*) Clues as to?

Ruth (*to Thomas*) That the evil had burrowed underground . . .

The woman DP sings a burst of a song of defiance, and goes.

Thomas (*to Ruth*) That was the first you heard?

Ruth (*of the icon*) 'Mother and Child'. Such fine brush strokes must have cost the painter his eyes. (*Holding out the icon to Theresa.*) Put it in the box.

Theresa The box has gone to the hospital with the sheets and the firewood.

Ruth (*to Thomas*) No, the first, we came to realise, was the duck lady, Anna of Lutsk, hunting for her little ones.

Thomas (*to Ruth*) So?

Ruth (*to Thomas*) So, to Dora, my deputy, a deeply moral person, to Theresa, not robust but so committed, and me I allocated villages to investigate some in the hills, some in the valley . . .

OUTSIDE THE BRANDAUERS' HOUSE 1945

Mr and Mrs Brandauer and a Priest.

Brandauer (*to Ruth*) I had two sons.

Thomas (*to Ruth*) Which village?

Ruth (*to Thomas*) First, Oberwössen.

Thomas On the crest of our hill.

Brandauer (*to Ruth*) Both my sons –

Priest (*to Ruth*) He had only sons.

Mrs Brandauer (*to Brandauer*) You think your feelings shame them? It gives them pleasure to hear it. Pastor, if you speak don't look at your feet.

Brandauer (*to Ruth*) Stalingrad!

Mrs Brandauer (*to Ruth*) Both our boys.

Priest (*to Ruth*) But every man has lost sons, there or elsewhere.

Brandauer (*to Ruth*) Now you feed foreigners, it's we who are suffering!

Mrs Brandauer (*to Ruth*) What do I have in my kitchen? Nothing but rats!

Brandauer (*to Ruth*) We plough our fields, what we harvest –

Priest (*to Ruth*) Your troops take it! How can you justify it, I ask you, morally?

Mrs Brandauer (*to the Priest*) Don't stare at your filthy feet!

Ruth (*to Thomas*) And back home through Hinterwössen – which was you.

Thomas Which was me.

THOMAS'S MOTHER'S HOUSE 1945

Ruth (*to Thomas's Mother*) A beautiful garden! How did you manage it during such upheavals? These lovely trailing flowers, nasturtiums we call them.

Thomas's Mother Oh, the sleepy ones, *Kapuzinerkresse*, orange, red, yellow, they get in everywhere, even where you'd never think to find them.

Ruth My mother adores them.

Thomas's Mother Your *mother*?

Ruth She has green fingers like you.

Thomas's Mother Tell her, seal the little fat seeds in a jar, in the spring close your eyes, do like this – (*Scattering.*) Up they come.

Ruth And this is your child's cat? Lazy fellow.

Thomas's Mother No, this is *my* good friend, Lotte.

Ruth Adorable. Come, pussy-pussy.

A ball is kicked on . . .

Ruth.

Thomas's Mother (*after a moment*) Susanne.

Ruth Yes, Susanne Hertzveld.

Thomas's Mother You have a record of our name?

Young Thomas appears. He is wearing glasses. Ruth kicks the ball back to him.

Thomas! Father is in the field, he needs you!

Young Thomas takes off his glasses and kicks the ball to Ruth. She returns it. He laughs.

Thomas's Mother I said, go to Father!

Young Thomas goes on playing.

Ruth Perhaps you were told when your crops ripen we'll take them. No. Our job is simply to find out if there are citizens of UN countries still working here, out of choice or . . .

Thomas's Mother We are three, no one more. My husband hunts rabbits, many nights we have no food, even for the child.

Ruth My dear, no need to conceal what you have.

Thomas's Mother I fear nothing, if I hide a jar of milk or some butter everyone in the village does the same.

While Young Thomas plays, his Mother tries to put his glasses on him. He resists.

Ruth Why do you insist, Mrs Hertzveld? (*To Young Thomas.*) May I?

She takes the glasses, looks through them.

He doesn't seem to need them.

Thomas's Mother Not to play, but when he reads me stories out of his book . . .

She ushers Young Thomas back into the house.

But why have you come to *my* house? You can see he is *not at all* a special child.

Thomas (*to Ruth*) You had a translator?

Ruth (*to Thomas*) Of course not, German is my language.

Thomas (*to Ruth*) But the raw Bavarian dialect . . . Did she really say *spezial*? Not another word, *bsundas* for example?

Thomas's Mother (*to Ruth*) To us he is everything.

THE SCHLOSS 1945

A common room. Night.

Theresa (*to Ruth*) Why bite her head off?

Ruth (*to Thomas*) If you want to check up, I'll drag my boxes from under Bill's bed, you can study the detailed notes I made on the spot.

Dora (*to Theresa*) Leave her.

Theresa (*to Dora*) Because?

Dora (*to Theresa*) She's frayed at the edges.

Theresa (*to Dora*) And how about *our* edges?

Ruth (*to Theresa*) In life you're an actress.

Theresa So?

Ruth What roles have you played?

Theresa Walk-ons.

Ruth That I could guess.

Theresa And Dorcas in *As You Like It*.

Ruth There is no such character in that play. But *you've* been trained to control your emotions.

Dora Oh, shut up about me. The world's vile, I'm right to be distressed.

Ruth (*to Dora*) Anger one can step out of clean but this emotional whirlpool . . .

Dora Where are my boots?!

Ruth 'Oh,' she says, '*we* uncovered nothing, how can you be certain there's a mystery to be solved?'

Theresa Somewhere there's barley sugar in a little round tin . . .

Dora You've found *one*, possibly, there's no evidence.

Ruth They were measuring children's noses, their genitals, great God in heaven!

Theresa (*to Ruth*) Have you gobbled it up? *Hast du meinen 'barley sugar' gegessen?*

Ruth (*to Dora*) Listen. When they showed us the instruments, what did we think about? The stolen children who failed the tests – oddly shaped noses, pigeon chests – but what of those who sailed through with flying colours? (*To Theresa.*) Yes. All of it. So what?

Theresa The whole tin?

Ruth (*to Dora*) What of children like little Thomas with perfect Aryan features . . . Oh. Is that it?

Theresa What?

Ruth Is his beauty the clue?

Dora (*weeping*) My stupid boots!

Ruth His perfection? Or am I chasing shadows? (*Of Dora.*) Oh, the Trevi Fountain, we must be in Rome, the Eternal City.

Theresa Please, Ruth.

Dora (*to Ruth*) Cow!

Theresa (*of the boots, to Dora*) Here, my love. (*To Ruth.*) Perhaps you've noticed, it's horridly late! (*To Dora.*) Why don't you stay?

Dora What, in the posh house with the Red Queen?

Ruth Pooh!

Theresa It's pelting down, we can share.

Dora Your *room*?

Theresa Silly, we're six, my bed. (*To Ruth.*) Good night, we're going up.

Ruth The child is long sighted, yes or no?

Theresa Tomorrow!

Dora *We* weren't at your tea party with Frau Marzipan.

Theresa (*to Dora*) Don't.

Dora *We* know nothing about it.

Theresa (*singing*) *Sleep tight* . . .

Dora He needs glasses, I wear glasses, what of it?

Ruth You've missed the point!

Theresa *The Sandman's on his way* . . .

Dora I'm Dora, I always miss the point!

Ruth (*laughing*) Oh, absolutely not at all.

She kisses her.

You, darling, win the Nobel Prize in insight and intuition.

Dora hugs her.

Theresa (*to Dora*) Let her go, she's a tar baby.

Ruth With his little foot, he makes his ball go wherever he pleases – ping! He pinged it to me, he could see exactly where I was standing.

Theresa Touch her, you'll never get away.

Ruth His glasses, I tried them on, the lens – very weak.

Theresa Come!

Ruth She says they're for him to read her stories. Then why shove them on his nose when he's playing football?

Dora Dear heart, he has poor eyesight, what am I missing?

Ruth But if he *seems* to have weak eyes, how can he be a perfect child?

Dora You said 'special'.

Theresa Enough!

Dora *Gute Nacht!* How's my accent?

Theresa No, don't, it's dark, the pavements are so broken up and uneven.

Dora I can walk across the yard and up the flipping lane. Where's my coat?

She goes outside.

Hoorah! The moon's out, a vast silver lake has flooded the heavens.

Theresa (*outside*) Ruth, come out, take a look.

Ruth goes outside.

Dora (*dancing in the moonlight*) Oh nature, all the evil in man rises to the stars, I'm washed clean by the moonlight, girls, I'm purity and goodness, la la la la la la.

Theresa (*to Ruth*) Margot Fonteyn.

Dora La la la la la la . . .

RUTH'S FLAT 1990

Ruth (*to Thomas*) But what did it *mean*, 'special'? Can it be the healthy blond boy in a comfortable home in fact belongs in a far-off land, his own little painted bed standing empty? It took us a while to adjust.

Thomas To?

Ruth The horror of it.

THOMAS'S MOTHER'S HOUSE 1945

Thomas's Mother (*handing George papers*) He is Thomas, born in Passau.

Ruth (*to George*) But does it *say* he was adopted?

George By Hertzveld, Wilfred and Susanne.

Ruth takes the papers.

Ruth 1940.

George At what age?

Ruth Wait . . . Yes, here. Almost five.

Thomas's Mother I was punished by God, unable to have my own.

Ruth (*sympathising*) My dear . . .

Thomas's Mother Not so close.

Ruth and George move away.

Ruth What was the protocol?

Thomas's Mother (*to George*) She means?

Ruth How did you come to have him?

Thomas's Mother (*to George*) Is it an order to tell her this?

Ruth Did you, for example, walk into some dormitory and say 'Not him with the pug nose, not him, his neck's too short'?

Thomas's Mother My husband signed papers, then more papers, at last our mayor –

Ruth Your mayor?

Thomas's Mother Made us a gift.

George And the boy's parents?

Thomas's Mother Dead, of course. And now God rewards me . . .

She reveals she is pregnant. Ruth recoils.

George (*to Ruth*) What's the matter with you?

RUTH'S FLAT 1990

Ruth (*to Thomas*) We possess nothing. Bill's awards for his photographs, prizes for my books – earthquakes, war can strip it all away. All that matters in this world is the suffering of others whoever they may be.

Thomas But all the same . . . ?

Ruth All the same, when I saw that woman's outrageous swollen belly . . .

Thomas You wanted to punish her?

Ruth Why does God punish the innocent? The cry of the ages.

Thomas You saw my mother as innocent?

Ruth It was Bavaria, Nazis were two a penny. I was enraged – what kind of devil infant would it be? Which was poppycock, a child is the world made new: that was, is, always will be my mantra.

Thomas But in the moment . . . ?

THOMAS'S MOTHER'S HOUSE 1945

Thomas's Mother So . . . ?

Ruth (*after a moment*) Heartfelt congratulations.

THE TOWN HALL 1945

Ruth, Dora, the Mayor.

Mayor (*short of breath*) Adoption papers for the district, not just my villages, all villages, are stored not here but in Passau.

Ruth Then, Mr Mayor, explain why two floors down in the foyer of your splendid town hall your assistant – such an enchanting smile which of course roused my suspicions . . .

Dora She was quite clear in those cabinets are all the documents we need.

Mayor We are closed for the day.

Ruth It's not even three!

Mayor Unfortunately.

AN OPTICIAN'S SHOP 1945

Ruth (*to Dora*) Tell Yannik we may be quite a long while at the optician so don't keep the car waiting, he should go find gas canisters and get his hair bobbed, make it easier to manage.

Dora But it's miles to walk back to the office. (*To the Optician.*) Excuse me!

Optician Moment.

Dora We've waited a colossally long time.

Optician Name.

Dora Happenstone, Dora.

Optician Of my patient about whom you wish information.

Dora Hertzveld.

Optician The father?

Dora The boy.

Optician Or the grandfather? Or one of the uncles? Half the village is Hertzveld.

Thomas Thomas Wulf Hertzveld.

A customer enters. The Optician hands Ruth a file, then sees to the customer.

(*To Dora.*) Get a look at other children, not only Hertzveld children, other children.

Ruth reads Young Thomas's file. Church bells toll.

(*To the Optician.*) What's the reason for this? It's not the hour, or the half.

Optician It's four on the dot.

Ruth (*showing her wristwatch*) Not at all.

Optician You trust that more than our thousand-year-old bells?

Dora looks through more files.

Ruth Doctor.

Optician (*to the customer*) Moment.

He goes to Ruth.

Ruth Do you know the expression 'special child'?

The Optician speaks to the customer, who leaves.

Optician To each mother her child is special. Not to mince words, Mrs Hertzveld has a deep love for her son, she brings him to me time and again. 'Doctor, do one more test, do another.' 'This is not a hobby, Susanne, like darts or carving spoons. If something is wrong, I'll find it . . .' But what she feels is, in my view, natural.

Thomas (*to Ruth*) Those glasses . . .

Ruth (*to the Optician*) In what way?

Optician An adopted child, a mother wants to be sure, will flaws come to the surface in later years?

Thomas (*to Ruth*) Made my head ache.

Optician She wants glasses for her child in case one day he needs them, is there harm in it? (*To Dora.*) Damn it, woman, did I give permission to rifle through every one of my files?

RUTH'S FLAT 1990

Ruth (*to Thomas*) The truth was the opposite of what the optician said. Your mother didn't fear you *may* have a flaw, every inch of your little body had been tested, she *knew* there wasn't one. She put glasses on your little nose to hide you, so your perfection wouldn't stand out amongst the other boys.

GEORGE'S OFFICE – EARLY EVENING 1945

Dora is handing out files. Theresa takes notes.

Theresa (*to George*) Once we persuaded Passau to release files –

George You should have come directly to my people. In this zone our authority is a hundred per cent.

Dora To get even *half*-truthful answers out of the villagers took weeks.

George (*to Ruth, of the Mayor*) For him, just headlines, keep it simple.

Ruth What is clear, Mr Mayor, is that very young children of Aryan appearance, infants in some cases, were plucked by trained personnel from newly conquered Slavic territories, brought to Germany *not to work* but to be tested to determine if they were (*reading*) 'genetically of value' or (*reading*) 'worthless'.

Dora (*of the files*) In one village, look – so many adopted children, taken from who knows where, all falsely registered 'born in Passau, born in Passau, Passau, Passau . . .'

George (*to the Mayor*) Why Passau?

Mayor I swear to God, I have not once put a foot in Passau.

Ruth Come, Mr Mayor, for me to get to Passau is twenty minutes and, as the highway is always cluttered with supply trucks and artillery wagons, I take country roads.

Mayor Passau is thirty thousand souls. In the war, must I explain, so many children were made orphans by your bombs. Our people have good hearts, they take them in.

Theresa (*offering Ruth a chair*) Sit.

Mayor (*to Ruth*) To you this is a crime? For what reason?

Ruth (*struggling for breath*) The reason, Mayor Huber, if you like reasons, that the UN is sited at Passau . . . Since the days of the Holy Roman Empire, Passau has been a seat of power with parade grounds, civic buildings . . .

She sits.

Which is why children were brought here to be 'processed' and, if they were deemed (*reading*) 'racially pure', parcelled out to Nazi Party members (*reading*) 'in good standing'.

Silence.

George (*to Theresa, of Ruth*) What's the matter with her?

Dora She won't eat.

Ruth I eat!

Dora Then vomits into the lavatory.

Silence.

(*To Ruth.*) Me then? (*To the Mayor.*) We were so boneheaded. These (*the files*) made it clear what happened to the darlings who passed the tests. And those who didn't? Behind the building where he found the instruments, through the yard, along a gravel path –

Mayor (*to George*) I was appointed mayor just two months ago under your regulations!

Dora Down steps, under the birch trees . . .

Mayor For this you must question my predecessor, Mayor Bülling.

George As we speak, my men are searching for Mayor Bülling village to village.

Dora The earth not even properly filled in.

RUTH'S FLAT 1990

Ruth (*to Thomas*) It was theatre on a gigantic scale. They'd lost millions and needed to replace them but, for the future, they wanted their troops to look superb in news reels – heroic profiles, godlike physiques.

GEORGE'S OFFICE – LATER THE SAME EVENING 1945

Theresa (*referring to a map*) Red circle here, here, here – our target villages.

Ruth (*to George*) We begin here.

Mayor Hinterwössen.

Ruth At first light.

Mayor Good, Councillor Hertzveld is highly respected, I will be with you.

George You will be in my headquarters under guard.

Mayor My country is an open wound. Are there even birds in the sky? My wife sees dead men walking.

Ruth (*to George*) Is he saying Hertzveld will resist?

Dora Let him!

THOMAS'S MOTHER'S HOUSE 1945

American soldiers surround the house. Bill takes photographs.

Thomas Father wasn't there. Mother tried to lock the door, she made me lie under the bed.

The American soldiers try to wrest Young Thomas from his mother; she struggles and cries out.

Ruth (*to the American Soldiers, of Thomas's Mother*) Let her go!

The American soldiers take Young Thomas and give him to Ruth. Distant rifle shots. Ruth hands Young Thomas to carers.

(*To Thomas.*) I was so clear in my mind what I was doing was right it seemed to me inevitable they would accept the new reality and –

Thomas (*to Ruth*) And what?

Bill takes a photograph of Ruth.

Ruth (*to Thomas*) Hand over the child. (*To Thomas's Mother.*) My dear . . .

Thomas's Mother slaps Ruth.

(*To Thomas.*) I feel it still.

OUTSIDE A ROOM IN THE SCHLOSS 1945

Sounds of distressed children from inside the room.

Ruth What am I hearing?

Theresa Are they praying?

Ruth Not at all. Are they? No.

Theresa (*to Ruth*) We don't use their names?

Ruth The sooner they forget them the better. Who shall we start with? Thomas?

Dora and Theresa laugh. Ruth slaps her wrist.

Ha! 'Wrong-headed Ruth'.

Theresa What names *do* we use?

Thomas (*to Ruth*) Some *were* praying, they were blubbering, whimpering. I ran down the corridor searching for you. *You* took me, so it was *you* who could take me back.

A Carer brings in Young Thomas.

Carer He wants to go home.

Young Thomas *Deaf I hoam iatzad? Bittschä?* [Can I go home now? Please?]

Ruth *Wir wissen nicht, wo dein Zuhause ist, Thomas.* [We don't know where your home is, Thomas.]

Dora and Theresa laugh.

Ruth (*to Dora and Theresa*) Oh, stop it.

She caresses Young Thomas's face.

Ah!

Theresa He bit you?

Ruth Not at all.

Theresa Let me see.

Young Thomas *I woas scho, wo I dahoam bi!* (*Cries.*) *Duat dränt!* [I know where my house is! It's over there!]

Dora (*to Young Thomas*) Brave heart, worn yourself to a rag, rest now, God's precious.

She tries to embrace him.

Young Thomas *Los mi gä! Do bist da Deifi!*

Young Thomas runs round trying to find a way out.

Ruth Oh really? I'm the devil.

Dora (*to Ruth*) We're all devils, he repeats what he hears, he doesn't mean it.

As Young Thomas shouts and curses, an American soldier tries to take hold of him.

Ruth Don't try to stop him! All the doors are locked, he'll wear himself out.

Young Thomas *I bring enk um oi mittanant!*

Theresa He wants to kill us all.

RUTH'S FLAT 1990

Thomas Ruth . . .

Ruth Do I go too far?

Thomas I've had almost no sleep.

Ruth Of course . . . The children's room is at the end of the corridor . . .

He goes out.

(*Calling.*) Open the window, let in some air . . .

ELISE'S HOUSE IN ALSACE 1945

Elise But what I can't *quite* fathom . . .

Ruth Oh, I can't go through it all again, *ma mère – what* don't you understand?

Elise It couldn't be simpler. Why you took the children.

Ruth (*after a moment*) I *still* reek from the train.

Elise Didn't I tell you brushing wouldn't do it? Slip it off, all of it. Marguerite! Quick, the girl will see to it.

Ruth No time, *maman.*

Elise She can wash them, they'll be dry by . . . Oh, you're *not* getting the evening train. Anyone can see you need rest.

Ruth I need to sleep a thousand years, I can't be doing with forty winks.

Elise Listen to me, when you're in bed and your eyes won't close, here's what to do – imagine you're shuffling a pack of cards.

Ruth Is that advice for Lady Macbeth, all night stalking the battlements? I'm drunk, pay no attention, I'm what the Yankees call *plotzed.*

Elise The *Yankees* call it *plotzed*?

Marguerite comes in.

(*To Ruth.*) Ah! Marguerite will bring you coffee. 'No, thank you.'

Ruth No, thank you.

Elise (*to Marguerite*) What can we do? It's her tradition, she refuses every comfort.

Marguerite goes.

Come look at the garden, come, the air's fresh after so much rain, though it was far less than we expected. Come.

THE SCHLOSS 1945

Young Thomas (*singing angrily*)
*Schlaf, Kindlein, schlaf
Der Vater hüt die Schaaf . . .*

OUTSIDE ELISE'S HOUSE IN ALSACE 1945

Ruth (*to Elise*) Last I saw you, you were there on the grass under the plum trees.

Elise *Quetsche d'Alsace.*

Ruth Kneeling, your yellow dress pulled up all the way.

Elise I hardly think so.

Ruth Your blue scarf draped over your shoulders, green gloves, putting in snowdrops. I can't see your nasturtiums . . .

Elise (*laughing*) Are you serious, at this time of year?

RUTH'S FLAT 1990

Thomas comes back into the room.

Ruth (*to Thomas*) You see, my mother was always right about *everything* – which young men to find appealing, which frocks to keep back for next season . . . I believed it must also be true of me.

Thomas (*to Ruth*) In what way?

Ruth (*to Thomas*) No matter how complicated the problem . . .

OUTSIDE ELISE'S HOUSE IN ALSACE 1945

Elise (*to Ruth*) Do you mean morally?

Ruth (*to Elise*) I feel something inside me is – don't laugh – so resolute, so serene –

Elise laughs.

So, what do *you* say we should do? Throw open the doors, let them scamper back down the hill to their wretched cottages? In Frankfurt we have teams of people searching day and night for their families. Will they find them? Or their parents might just show up in Passau . . . We don't fucking know.

Elise To your mother you show your unvarnished side, not attractive.

Ruth I came for advice.

Elise A wasted journey.

Ruth I'll go.

Elise It stares one in the face. Take them back, leave them with the women who, whatever the reality, *seem to them* to be their mothers . . .

Thomas (*to Ruth*) Did she say that?

Elise (*to Ruth*) My dear, what is it? A cramp?

Ruth Bowels.

Elise Inside, go, go!

Thomas Ruth.

Ruth (*to Elise*) What is it with you? You never let me finish a single sentence! (*To Thomas.*) What!?!

Thomas (*to Ruth*) Lying on your bed, I remembered something warm, a furry creature . . .

Ruth (*to Thomas*) Your mother's cat. When we fetched you, it sat on your lap in the jeep. We took it back.

Elise (*laughing*) The *cat* you took back? Let me feel your forehead, you have an infection?

Ruth (*to Elise*) No, it's fear, naked fear. *Maman*, the truth.

Elise My darling . . .

Ruth Have I done something wrong?

Elise To a stupendous degree! It's a calamity! Don't believe me, the evidence will be the fury of the people whose future you're stealing. Stay the night, tomorrow go back, put a stop to it.

Ruth That you are my mother –

Elise Who loves you.

Ruth That gives you no right to give me orders.

Elise Ah, idiot. You asked me!

Ruth A wrong has been done.

Elise You are doing it.

Ruth I follow an inner light!

OUTSIDE THE SCHLOSS 1945

Father, drunk, wearing a German army uniform, brandishes a rifle.

Thomas's Father *Wo isa denn mei Thomas, ha?* [Where is my Thomas?]

Young Thomas *Data!* [Father!]

Thomas's Father *Wo bisdn, mei Bua?* [Where are you, my boy?]

Young Thomas *Do bini, Datta! Hoi mi assi!* [I'm here, father! Save me!]

Thomas's Father *Kapåin fangt s Spuin o. Da Haupmann: 'Wirf deinen Spaten weg, es ist einfachen Soldaten verboten, auch nur ein Schützenloch zu graben.'* [The band begins. The captain: 'Throw away your spade, it is forbidden for ordinary soldiers to dig even one foxhole.']

Young Thomas *I kim!* [I'm coming!]

Thomas's Father *I fang d'Kugl af mit maina nockadn Brust!* [I'll take the bullet in my naked breast!]

Thomas's Father fires his rifle. American soldiers knock him down. Young Thomas is there.

Ruth (*to the American soldiers*) No, no, leave him! You don't need to . . . !

The American soldiers back off.

Come, Councillor Hertzveld, we'll easily sort this out. (*To Young Thomas.*) Young man.

Young Thomas *Jo?*

Ruth *Wer ist dieser feine Kerl?* [Who is this fine fellow?]

Young Thomas *Des is mei Datta.*

Ruth *Dein Vater? Was sollen wir tun, damit es ihm besser geht? Was mag er? Weißt du das? Mag er Bier? Es scheint so. Ich hole welches und du kannst es ihm geben. Aber zuerst sollten wir ihm das Gewehr wegnehmen, das ist gesunder Menschenverstand, nicht so? Hilfst du mir dabei?* But first we should take the gun away, that's common sense, right? Will you help me with it? [Your father? What shall we do to make him feel better? What does he like? Do you know? Does he like beer? It seems so. I'll fetch some and you can give it to him.]

Young Thomas helps Ruth gently take the rifle from his Father. He disarms it. Ruth helps Thomas's Father get up. American soldiers take him away.

Young Thomas *Datta!*

Young Thomas dashes about until he's exhausted and alone with Ruth.

Ruth *Komm! Oder komm nicht.* Choose, my little one. Come to me or don't come. Up to you.

He goes to her and lies in her arms.

And if your eyes won't close, here's what you do: imagine you're shuffling a pack of cards.

Act Three

RUTH'S FLAT 1990

The room is darker than before.

Thomas I'm on stage in front of an audience . . . It happened without warning. I was playing Rachmaninoff –

He plays a few notes.

– at maximum speed held high above myself, if you see what I mean, up near the ceiling, by rolling chromatic waves.

He plays.

Someone floated into my mind. Who? I play too loud, my God, I'm banging, my manager, Gisela, standing in the wings, puts her hands over her face.

He plays.

'I swear,' I told her, 'it will never happen again!' I began to get bookings in the capitals of Europe, top-tier halls, where perhaps by chance the someone – she, her – might wander in . . . I'd fix on one of the mid-price seats . . . I didn't even know in which city you live, but is she there?

Ruth I'm here . . .

Thomas Is she listening?

Ruth I'm listening . . .

Thomas One day . . . Bach –

He plays.

– what's going on? I'm skating over the notes, I'm making it up, I'm lost – help! – it's terrifying. I find my way back, modulating through key after key, the end. And then the applause . . . Gisela kisses my forehead, helps me out of my seat. And now . . .

Ruth And now it's what you do. You found your artistic soul. Good for you.

Thomas A theme –

He plays a few notes.

I elaborate . . .

He plays.

It takes stupendous energy, absence of mind, sheer being, every experience I've ever had flowing through my fingers . . . The crisis, or the change, happened years before I found you when I'd no idea, how could I, if you were even in the land of the living . . . I prayed, tell the truth, you were not.

Ruth Charming.

Thomas That you were dead.

Ruth Sorry to disappoint.

Thomas I knew, somehow, if I ever bumped into you, let's say on an underground train, I'd be finished.

He refills his glass.

Or I prayed *I* was dead so there could be no chance of it. Though, all these years, I longed for you. I dashed out of the park, ran up your stairs – I upset you, I'm sorry.

Ruth Not at all. Tell me, simple words, what the hell happened?

Thomas My head exploded, I needed to be clear.

Ruth Then be clear.

Thomas You said it was chance you were 'grounded' in Passau not far from my village.

Ruth I injured my foot.

Thomas Yes, but why *you*?

Ruth Why me?

Thomas Why *that* village?

Ruth No, your question, if you'll let me get a word in, (*laughing*) is why *you*?

Thomas (*laughing*) It was never about me! I was some Kraut kid you pulled up by the roots, found not to your taste and flung back.

Ruth So, the reason for your visit – no, we need, as you say, to be clear – is to punish me.

Thomas Ten years ago, Gisela – 'I've just read a book about your part of the world.' 'Oh?' 'A memoir.' 'Oh?'

Ruth Not a peep out of you in three decades then, care of my German publisher, a postcard – I have it . . .

Thomas You do?

Ruth Of course, in my hefty 'Thomas Hertzveld' file. Tiny writing all down one side – 'How is it that a long book about *my*, underlined, country, *my* life turns out to be –'

Thomas (*laughing*) All about you!

Ruth This is childish, which may be a good thing, but . . . If the story of my '"marvellously audacious life" – *The Times*' is nothing but ego, why knock on my door?

Thomas Today?

Ruth (*beaming at him*) Fool, no, in the old house, Bill's sixtieth as it happened, now he's seventy, you turn up cool as a cucumber – wait! – out of the blue, for an hour you sing Handel arias, falsetto, all of us, including the children, dance in the street making it, so Bill always tells me, his most joyous ever birthday though I, of course, saw through the high spirits.

Thomas What did you see?

Ruth (*after a moment*) Years go by, you don't even return my phone calls. Each of your recordings, as it comes out, is added to the shelf.

Thomas Is that true?

Ruth I keep them in the order they were released.

Thomas But do you also listen to them?

Ruth (*in tears*) Why can you not believe I love you? No, you've said a mouthful. My turn. What I'm doing today, I give you my word, is spilling the beans.

She refills his glass.

You may need it. Where was I sitting? Wait a moment. Good. Allow me to approach our subject –

Thomas Which is?

Ruth Moral responsibility. From a different angle. You ask why did I take you back to Susanne. You lived with her how many years? I've no reason to believe – and, of course, I've given this much thought – that you were unhappy there. After you left for the US, in '54, was it?

Thomas Is this research for another memoir?

Ruth You were nineteen, many youngsters leave home far earlier, it couldn't have been as rough as all that.

Thomas My life in Hinterwössen. For a start, who was I?

Ruth Thomas Wulf Hertzveld.

Thomas But whose blood was in my veins?

Ruth Oh, come now. 'Blood', indeed.

Thomas With no genetic link to my so-called parents –

Ruth Why 'so-called'?

Thomas What sort of beast would I become?

Ruth They loved you and brought you up –

Thomas Would I be tall or short?

Ruth A sensitive –

Thomas Smart or stupid?

Ruth Talented –

Thomas My father, his rage, no, disappointment – with me, and with history . . . But when he beat me, had he any right to do it? My instincts, could I trust them, what *could* I trust? Is that *my* flower garden, *my* hunting rifle, *my* sky, or will it all be taken from me *again*? When I got my scholarship to Tampa, Florida, I stayed away fifteen years.

Ruth But during all that time you kept in close touch with Susanne, long letters, tiny handwriting, or am I wrong?

Thomas I only went 'home' because my sweet, passionate, illiterate mother was ill, dying actually, but the question that brought me here from New York –

Ruth Yes, what you bellowed as you stormed through the door with an, as yet, unexplained urgency is why, when you were ten years old, did I take you back to her.

Thomas But behind that is another question . . .

Ruth Why did I take you from her in the first place?

Thomas No!

Ruth Then what? Why didn't *I* keep you?

Thomas God, Ruth. *Why didn't you keep me?*

THE SCHLOSS 1945

Ruth is holding Young Thomas between wakefulness and sleep. Dora and Theresa sew children's clothes. The Cook is cooking. Bill, an American army photographer, is preparing his equipment.

Bill (*to Ruth*) What you're putting out is all your pint-sized Siegfrieds and Brünnhildes are *not* German, *not* German. Is that it?

Dora (*to Ruth*) Shall I . . . ? (*To Bill.*) The evidence –

Bill Oh, there's evidence? Gotcha.

Ruth (*to Thomas*) There's so much I could say.

Theresa (*to Bill*) Adoption certificates, remarkably detailed records . . .

Bill So, it's all hunky-dory and on the level?

Theresa (*to Bill*) Yes, and . . . Ruth?

Dora (*to Theresa*) You can tell him, none of it's classified information.

Ruth (*to Thomas*) We took the bold, even brutal but necessary step, but as to what would happen next . . .

Theresa (*to Bill*) Other children, cases very like ours –

Dora (*to Bill*) Identical!

Theresa (*to Bill*) – have turned up in other centres.

Ruth (*to Thomas*) Our moral responsibility was to find out where you come from, who you are.

Bill Be happy, ladies.

Ruth (*to Bill*) I am extraordinarily happy.

Bill I'll make each of your kids look a million bucks.

Ruth It's not a beauty parade. All we ask – Bill, kindly pay attention – is a sharply defined image so that, though years may have gone by, their mothers –

Bill You're saying you'd prefer my photographs to be in focus?

Ruth And keep the framing simple – here's an attractive little girl, here's an appealing young boy . . .

Bill Well, I've been using this Speed Graphic with the 203mm Kodak Anastigmatic lens – ideal, I always think, for portraits but it weighs half a ton and there's how many to shoot? So, I could use the lovely Leica but this is far from the latest, it's pre-war, to state the obvious.

Ruth (*to Thomas*) Basic protocols were obvious – take photographs of each child, send them to the Central Tracing Bureau near Frankfurt.

Bill (*to Ruth*) In fact, I've been planning to finagle a week's R&R, catch a ride to Wetzlar, wherever that is, and pick up the latest model though whether the Leica team have gone on refining all the gizmos given recent, possibly more urgent, manufacturing priorities . . .

He points his camera at Ruth.

Dora Don't, she won't allow it.

Ruth (*adjusting her hair*) Why not, if it's for official purposes?

Bill (*to Ruth*) How is it the Kaiser's nephew gets front row seats? I'll do his down the line, this is you.

Theresa takes Young Thomas and sits him at the table. While Bill photographs Ruth, the Cook gives Young Thomas bread and milk.

He's not yours, is he?

Ruth In what way mine?

Bill How many ways are there?

Thomas Plenty.

Ruth (*to Thomas*) But apart from that, in terms of what *then* we should actually *do* . . .

Theresa sits next to Young Thomas.

Young Thomas (*screaming at Theresa*) *Do hock di ned hi! Nem meina sitzt oiwei mei Mam.*

Ruth (*to Thomas*) We were at sea.

Theresa Strange, he seems to be keeping a place for his mother.

Dora (*to Ruth*) She's not coming, is she?

Ruth (*harshly*) Of course she isn't.

Dora (*to Ruth*) But do we condone violent behaviour?

Thomas eats.

Bill Ruth, look up.

Ruth Oh please.

Bill Look down.

Ruth Like so?

Bill Look through the back of your head.

Ruth *So* amusing.

Bill Look into the light.

Ruth I always do!

Theresa (*holding up a piece of bread*) Let's try this. (*To Young Thomas.*) 'Bread'. In Polish *chleb*.

Everyone watches Thomas.

No? *Chleb. Chl-eb* . . . Okay, in Russian *khleb*. No? In Ukrainian *khlib*.

Cook Say magic words, you believe the little ones will jump out of a box like a clown in the circus, big kiss, 'Hello, Miss America.'

Ruth We're not American.

Bill Speak for yourself.

Theresa holds up a glass of milk.

Theresa 'Milk'.

Ruth (*to Thomas*) In the thirties, Piaget had published on child language acquisition.

Theresa Polish *mleko*. Russian *moloko*.

Ruth (*to Thomas*) We knew nothing.

Theresa Ukrainian also *moloko*.

Cook Ach, he's only pretending to swallow. Ugly brat! Chew with your wolf's teeth!

Young Thomas vomits at her.

Pig! Demon!

Ruth (*to the Cook*) You do not shout at him!

Cook (*aiming a slap at him*) Heathen!

Ruth (*to the Cook*) You do not hit him! Where did we dig you up? Who were you working for?

Dora What *I* wish . . . What *I* wish on this balmy afternoon is we were boiling up enormous urns of raspberries, stirring in bags of lovely sugar with a long spoon . . .

The sounds of children crying . . .

THE SCHLOSS 1945 – ANOTHER DAY

Ruth (*to Young Thomas*) *Mein kleiner Liebling, ich bin ganz sicher, dass du einen wahren Namen hast, den du im Herzen trägst.* [My little darling, I am quite certain you have a true name which you hold in your heart.]

Theresa (*to Dora*) She's asking him to think hard and his 'true name', *wahren Namen* –

Dora *Wahren Namen.*

Theresa Will pop out of his heart.

Ruth *Stell dir vor, du bist in deinem Bett, eingewickelt in eine 'woolly blanket'.*

Theresa (*simultaneous*) Imagine you're in your bed wrapped in a woolly blanket.

Ruth (*to Theresa*) Stop mumbling!

Theresa I never do, and don't you snap!

Dora Oh, darlings . . .

RUTH'S FLAT 1990

Thomas (*furious, to Ruth*) But did it never occur to you . . . ? When we arrived in 'our new homeland' – it's hard to say – so frightened, everything upside down, utterly bewildered, if we uttered one word in our own language we were whipped.

Ruth (*to Thomas*) Not by Susanne.

Thomas (*to Ruth*) Of course not by Susanne!

Ruth (*to Thomas*) By who?

Thomas (*to Ruth*) Did I ever even see their face . . . ?

Dora Everyone, come now, deep breaths – in, out . . . The Salvation Army cure for all trials and afflictions.
(*Singing.*)
'What a friend we have in Jesus . . .'

Theresa interrupts Dora with a Ukrainian song. Young Thomas interrupts Theresa with a German marching song.

Children *Sie ist da! Sie ist gekommen! Mama! Das ist meine Mama!* [She's there! She's come! Mama! It's my mama!]

Dora (*looking through the window*) Look at her running through the field upsetting the horses.

Theresa Who is it this time?

Dora Her from Lutsk. *Via!* Go away! *Weg! Weg.* (*Calling.*) Anna, you know your children aren't here!

Translator (*simultaneously*) *Anna, ty znayesh, shcho tvoyikh ditey tut nemaye.*

Theresa She's my all-time hero, she'll never give up.

Dora (*through the window*) Yes, poor you, but you're not allowed in these grounds!

Ruth Quick, ask if she has any ducks, we could do with a good dinner for once. Fat ones! Quack quack.

Translator (*calling*) *U vas ye kachky na prodazh . . . ?*

Ruth (*laughing*) Don't translate that!

Theresa I'll go down, me she trusts. I don't make jokes about her, and I don't have favourites.

She goes.

Ruth (*to Thomas*) And then . . .

RUTH'S FLAT 1990

Ruth fetches her 'Thomas Hertzveld' file, takes out drawings, gives them to Thomas . . .

THE SCHLOSS 1945 – ANOTHER DAY

Bill So, what's in *my* wooden head . . . Alright then, I'm lining up a shot, what sticks in my mind is the image – distance to horizon, angle of sun . . . Do I remember *when* I took it, the day, even the year . . . ? (*To the Cook.*) What's this?

Cook Black Forest marshmallow pudding cake.

Bill Perhapz memory iz . . .

He turns the cake upside down.

Like zo!

Dora (*laughing*) What on earth?

Bill Now ve can zee vot liez deep at ze bottom . . .

Ruth (*to Thomas*) Bill.

Bill Iz memory perhaps layer beneath layer, cherriez, martzmellow, each layer melting into ze ozzer, nutz, cuztard, tzinnamon . . . But seriously, folks, could it be deep inside *their* heads they have layer on top of layer of images – a wooden toy, a sycamore outside a window . . . ? What've you got for them to play with? No, that's no good, here we are. Hey, Tommy!

He gives Young Thomas paper and crayons.

RUTH'S FLAT 1990

Thomas is looking through drawings he did forty years ago.

THE SCHLOSS 1945

Bill (*to Ruth*) Suggest he draws something, anything, he remembers.

Ruth (*to Young Thomas*) *Woran kannst du dich erinnern, Thomas? Warum versuchst du nicht, das zu zeichnen?* [What can you remember, Thomas? Why not try drawing that?]

They watch Young Thomas drawing.

Dora (*to Bill*) Shouldn't we give him clearer instructions?

Young Thomas takes a new piece of paper.

Bill Yes, the lady's right about that. Tell him draw what he feels strongly about . . .

Ruth (*to Bill*) You're sure?

Dora Trust me. (*To Young Thomas.*) My love, what comes into your mind if I say . . .

Ruth (*simultaneous*) *Was fühlst du, wenn ich sage . . .*

Dora Christmas cake.

Bill No, I mean something that really churned up his guts.

Ruth watches Thomas looking at picture after picture and at Young Thomas drawing.

Cook And tomorrow trucks come and take them all back to their mothers, *ja?*

She goes.
   Young Thomas gives a drawing to Ruth and goes with Dora. Ruth looks at it, then hands it to Thomas. Bill goes. Thomas looks at the drawing.

THE SCHLOSS 1945

Night. Ruth asleep.

Theresa (*offering Ruth a cup*) Take it.

Ruth (*tasting it*) Cocoa! You're waking me to help me get to sleep? Where from?

Theresa Your 'friend'.

Ruth Bill brought enough for everyone? No? Then we share it. I stink with sweat. Tell me.

Dora (*to Ruth*) We've made a serious error.

Ruth In whose opinion?

Dora They're so German, everything they do, how they do it.

Theresa Thomas came up with a name.

Ruth But that's wonderful.

Theresa It's from so deep in his memory, he can't remember whose it is.

Ruth All that matters is what language!

Dora German!

Theresa It's the name of a German woman.

Dora So, he must actually *be* German.

Ruth What is the name?

Dora Listen to us for once, dear.

Ruth What German woman?

Dora We've been ill-advised.

Theresa Lotte.

Thomas laughs.

Ruth Lotte is his mother's cat! Puss-puss, Susanne Hertzveld's cat!

They all laugh.

RUTH'S FLAT 1990

Ruth (*to Thomas*) But the wiliest wasn't Dora, certainly not Theresa or even Bill . . .

THE COURTYARD OF THE SCHLOSS 1945

George and American soldiers arrive with Young Thomas, a beachball, baseball bats . . .

George (*to Ruth, of Young Thomas*) Is it agreeable to kidnap this piglet?

Dora Oh, my forefathers, no – but where do you boys want to take him?

American Soldier 1 (*picking up Young Thomas*) To the river!

American Soldier 2 (*to Young Thomas*) Don't poop your pants, we only eat plump piglets.

Dora (*to Ruth*) Oh, can we go with them?

Theresa No. Ruth . . . ?

American Soldier 1 (*to Young Thomas*) Hey, *tovarich, vy Russki? Vy Russki,* Thomas? [Are you Russian, Thomas?]

American Soldier 2 He's not. I know. My mom, my pop –

American Soldier 3 His sexy sisters.

American Soldier 2 – are full-blood Russkies from the mountains of Arkansas!

American Soldier 3 *I'm* a Pole, (*of Young Thomas*) he's a Polack, that one's a greaseball.

Dora (*to Ruth*) Can we, Ruth?

American Soldier 3 Oh sure, we'll take them all!

American Soldier 2 All the kids or all the babes?

Theresa (*to Ruth*) Well, I'm not going.

American Soldier 1 (*to Theresa*) Do you know even the basic rules of baseball?

The American soldiers play ball with Young Thomas. Bill takes photographs.

American Soldier 2 Hey, why don't we pack him in a suitcase when we go home?

American Soldier 1 No, my little woman is aiming for one of her own.

American Soldier 2 But here you can take them off the shelf.

American Soldier 1 Me, I'm into DIY.

American Soldier 2 Hey, kid, can you do this?

He stands on his head, etc.

Try! I'll hold you . . .

American Soldier 3 pretends to point a pistol at Young Thomas.

American Soldier 3 Stop foolin' and tell us your name.

Theresa (*to Ruth, of American Soldier 3*) I told you . . .

American Soldier 3 (*to Young Thomas*) I'll count to five.

Ruth (*to American Soldier 3*) Don't do that! George!

George (*to American Soldier 3*) Moron! (*To Young Thomas.*) Hey, kiddo!

He runs about like a dog.

Look, puppy dog, what does it *do*? An itchy, scratchy pooch? Woof!

The American soldiers bark and act like dogs. Young Thomas barks like a dog.

Hey, tickle my whiskers, he had a dawg! Now we're getting somewhere. What was the hound's name, kiddo?

George, the American soldiers and Young Thomas go off to the river . . .

Ruth Dora . . .

Dora goes, then Theresa goes too.

Sound of Children *Das ist großartig, ich kann ewig unter Wasser bleiben, spritz mir nicht ins Gesicht, atme, atme!* [This is great, I can stay underwater forever, don't splash in my face, breathe, breathe!]

Bill So, with all this thinking about how to find happy endings for the kiddies –

Ruth Don't call them that.

Bill Don't it cross your mind *you* might like to, perhaps, at some point, skedaddle off too?

Ruth Not at all.

Bill Not at no point never?

Ruth This is my work, kindly treat it with respect.

Bill Got it.

Ruth The truth is I've barely got going.

Bill Hell of a thing.

Ruth When I came here . . .

Bill Direct from DC?

Ruth As you're well aware.

Bill Must have been tough.

Ruth Not tough enough.

Bill You don't say?

Ruth What I longed for, what I imagined I'd find, was work so arduous –

Bill Physical work?

Ruth I'd be overwhelmed.

Bill Hell of a thing.

Ruth Crushed even.

Bill Because there are so many hideous Huns for you to beat up on?

Ruth I wish to 'beat up on' nobody except you Yankees for 'hollering' –

Bill Oh, we sure can holler.

Ruth That the only place our 'kiddies' –

Bill The whole posse or your particular Siegfried?

Ruth Thomas isn't mine. Don't bat your eyelids. 'Hollering' that the only place our children should be taken is 'freedom-loving USA'.

Bill You'd prefer they grow up slaves to Bolshevik collective-hoodad what's it-ism?

Ruth Each child will be safely returned to their own home.

Bill Yes, sweets, that's got into my wooden head, but 'crushed by work', what's the reason? It doesn't seem to have happened, by the way.

Ruth To find out what I'm made of.

Bill Hell of a thing.

Ruth Ever since I was a child, I've felt I have something –

Bill You do.

Ruth Inside . . .

Bill Something unique?

Ruth A sort of nugget.

Bill Is this a medical condition?

Ruth It can't be broken up or melted down, it must be handed on.

Bill To who? Whom. To whom must it be handed on?

Ruth I hope one day to discover.

George, the American soldiers, Young Thomas, Theresa and Dora come on.

George Hey, Ruth!

Bill (*to Ruth*) Hey, sweets, how's about yours truly?

Ruth What's happened? Thomas?

Bill Ruth?

American Soldier 3 I did it, I'll tell it.

Bill (*to Ruth*) How about me?

George He asked him in Polish language what was his dog's name.

American Soldier 3 I was all playful like to loosen him up. Thomas, *jak wabił sie twój pies'?* What was your dog's name? And he says . . . Say it, buddy. *Powiedz im, młody!* Woof? *Młody?*

Young Thomas *Słonko.*

Silence.

American Soldier 3 I'm telling you, lady, I'm Polish from a village outside Rzeszów and that's my language he's talking.

Ruth What does it mean?

George Seems he had a pooch name of Słonko.

American Soldier 3 Słonko bein' a name Polish people give a pooch. It means sunbeam, sun-fuckin'-beam!

Ruth Say it, Thomas.

George Say it, Tommy boy . . .

Young Thomas (*after a moment, laughing*) Słonko! Słonko!

American Soldiers *Słonko! Słonko! Słonko!*

Young Thomas (*laughing*) Słonko! Słonko! Słonko! Słonko!

Bill takes photographs of Young Thomas.

Young Thomas (*to Ruth*) Popatrz na mnie!

American Soldier 3 See what we've done! He's unstoppable! *Popatrz na mnie* is 'look at me'!

Young Thomas (*posing for the camera*) Popatrz na mnie! Patrz! Patrz! [Look! Look!]

American Soldier 3 (*to Ruth*) It's every word top class Polish, by the way.

RUTH'S FLAT 1990

Ruth (*to Thomas*) Word flew round the villages. Thomas is a Pole! It was as though a dam burst, scribbled notes appeared on my desk – 'Meet me where no one will see us, behind the railway station . . .'

THE HILLSIDE 1945

Ruth '. . . or on the crest of the hill.' I picked daffodils and snow-white daisies.

Gertrude holds a child's suitcase.

Gertrude I told many lies.

Ruth My dear, to punish yourself helps no one.

As Gertrude hands Ruth the suitcase, a young girl's clothes spill out.

Gertrude Take it now, all, or I grab it and run.

Ruth examines the clothes . . .

She speaks as we do but, sleeping, she makes blah blah.

Ruth She talks in her sleep? Can you tell what language it is?

Gertrude At first, I was afraid even to touch her. If water comes out her mouth, will it make me ill?

Ruth No one doubts that you love her, no one.

Ruth packs the clothes into the suitcase. Gertrude takes the flowers.

Gertrude At night she sleeps on the side of her heart, it's dangerous, I don't allow it.

She goes.

THE CENTRAL TRACING BUREAU, AROLSEN 1945

Chief Researcher (*to Ruth*) Trains running smoothly now, are they? It's unusual for officers to make their way to Frankfurt. By and large, photographs arrive by what we call donkey post, and they do, in their thousands, photos, of course, but pencil sketches done from memory . . . You have a name?

Ruth hands the Chief Researcher a file.

Ruth Excuse my appalling writing.

Chief Researcher Lola Krawczyk.

The Chief Researcher hands the file to other researchers who look through the records.

How'd you come across it?

Ruth It was sewn into the waistband of her knickers.

Chief Researcher Remarkable. Actually, we've had quite a few of those. Some children even managed somehow to keep hold of books, prayer books mostly, that had their names clearly marked on the title page. Oh, and some names we've found scratched onto the soles of shoes.

Researcher Krawczyk Bohdan, Krawczyk Pawel . . .

Chief Researcher Popular name, it seems.

Researcher Krawczyk Andrzej . . .

Chief Researcher Not to dampen expectations but, our experience, though Krawczyk is Polish it doesn't inevitably follow that *Miss Lola* Krawczyk was actually born in . . .

Researcher I have a Mrs Grzegorz Krawczyk of Lubelskie province. File opened February seventeenth.

She hands the file to the Chief Researcher.

Chief Researcher Mrs Grzegorz Krawczyk – keen to have young Lola back it seems.

She hands Ruth the letter from the file.

And the picture of Lola they sent.

She hands her a photograph.

Handsome woman, the mother, don't you think?

RUTH'S FLAT 1990

Ruth (*to Thomas*) Our Hildegard – Agata . . . Our little Gunther – Mykola . . .

Thomas And Klaus was in fact Fyodor, Anna-Maria was Katarzyna and, and, and . . .

THE SCHLOSS 1945

Young Thomas smashes a plate. The carers surround Ruth to protect her.

George Tell the little faker – one more time, I'll kick his skinny ass.

Ruth *Thomas, wovor hast du Angst?* [Thomas, what are you afraid of?]

Theresa (*to Ruth*) Is he afraid you won't find out who he is?

Dora (*to Ruth*) Or that someone will come and take him from you?

Theresa (*to Dora*) No, surely he *wants* to go home.

Young Thomas smashes a second plate.

George Game over! Everyone out! Vamoose!

Ruth smashes a plate. Young Thomas laughs.

Dora This is lunacy!

Young Thomas holds up a plate. Ruth holds up a plate.

Now stop it, my darlings, both of you.

Theresa All the children will start, no one will be safe . . .

Dora Plates are for eating scrumptious food. *Schatz,* is that the word?

George This ends now!

Dora Come to Dora, *mein Schatz.*

Ruth (*to Young Thomas*) *Aber wenn du stark bist, stark hier drin, dann habe ich etwas für dich.* [But if you have strength, inner strength, I have something for you.]

Theresa Oh good, if he's strong she'll give him something to calm him down. (*To Ruth.*) Is that what you mean?

Ruth *Und nur für dich allein.* [And only for you.]

Young Thomas *Wos håstn fia mi?* [What have you got for me?)

Dora (*to Ruth*) You're not going to bribe him?

Young Thomas (*screaming*) *Jest już ciemno!*

Dora Now what fool language is he speaking?

Translator It's Polish. 'Already the sky is dark outside.'

Ruth (*to the Translator*) Ask him . . .

Translator Tell me.

Ruth If he could have anything, the furthest star, a jewel from the ocean bed, what would it be?

Translator (*simultaneous*) *Gdybyś mógł sobie czegoś życzyć, najodleglejszej z gwiazd, skarbu z głebin oceanu, co by to było?*

Young Thomas *Mei Nåchtessn wuii!* (I want my tea.)

Ruth *Nåchtessn* . . . Your tea! Of course! It's dark, your tea time. *Was gibt es zum Nåchtessn?* No! (*To the Translator.*) In Polish. 'What do you have for tea?'

Translator *Co jadasz na podwieczorek?*

Young Thomas *Chleb.*

Translator Polish. Bread.

Young Thomas *Kromka z miodem.*

Translator A slice of bread with honey.

Carers bring bread and honey.

Young Thomas *Nie, ty! Ty mi to day!* [No, you! You give it to me!]

Ruth makes Thomas a honey sandwich.

Moja mama piecze chleby, miód mojego taty jest najlepszy na świecie.

Translator His accent is pure Galicia, Poland south-east. 'My mother bakes the best bread, my father's honey is the finest in the world.'

Ruth (*to Young Thomas*) Is your father's honey the finest because it comes from deep in the forest?

Translator *Czy to dlatego, że pochodzi z głębi lasu?*

Young Thomas *Nie, nasze ule sa na dachu stajni dla koz.*

Translator No, our beehive is on the roof of the goat shed.

Everyone laughs.

Ruth (*to Young Thomas*) Goat shed – *stajni?*

Young Thomas *Na dachu stajni dla koz.*

Ruth And how do you say bees?

Young Thomas (*to the Translator*) *Co?* [What?]

Translator *Pyta, jak powiedzieć 'pszczoły'.* ([he wants to know how to say 'bees'.]

Young Thomas *Dlaczego?* [Why?]

Translator *Nie wiem. Po prostu rób, co Ci mówi.* [I don't know. Just do what she says.]

Young Thomas (*laughing*) *Pszczoły.*

Ruth *Psz . . . ?*

Young Thomas (*teaching her*) *Pszczoły! Psz-czo-ły! Pszczoły!*

Everyone *Pszczoły!*

Act Four

RUTH'S BEDROOM IN THE SCHLOSS 1945

Ruth lays the exhausted Young Thomas on a bed.

Dora And if we find out nothing more about him?

Ruth Don't do that.

Dora (*laughing*) What do I do?

Ruth Bully me.

Dora Ever so gently.

Theresa He's sleeping like an angel.

Ruth Why is everyone so convinced I want him?

Dora Oh, you want nothing. Your clothes in rags, your bed hard as nails, you eat no more than we give the DPs. By taking nothing, oldest story in the world, you get everything.

Ruth What do I get?

Dora Pride in the greatness of your soul, how luminous it is.

After a moment, Ruth embraces Dora. Young Thomas is watching.

(*To Ruth.*) You're hot, let me feel. Is it your heart? Child, we all see how you look at him. Theresa lives by the rules, to form attachments to one's charges is sin number one.

Theresa But it is!

Dora He was your first. You took him with these hands.

Ruth In my mind I'm flint, I'm straw blown by the wind. When it seems I could keep him, even should, who comes into my mind?

Dora *Ta mère.*

Ruth My mother.

Dora What of her?

Ruth Her house overlooks a lagoon. War came, she sat on her porch under her straw hat, went nowhere, did nothing.

Dora She brought you up and, if she has faults, you more than make up for it.

Young Thomas *Wos schnodastn do umanant?*

Ruth (*to Dora*) 'What are we jabbering about?' (*To Young Thomas.*) *Meine Mutti.*

Young Thomas *Wo isn de dahoam?*

Dora 'Where does she live?' Yes?

Ruth *Nicht weit von hier. Normalerweise, einen Tag mit dem choo-choo.* [Not far from here. In ordinary times, one day in a train.]

Theresa (*to Dora*) Her mother lives one day away.

Dora (*ironically*) Oh?

Young Thomas *Mei Mam is oiwei bei mia.*

Ruth I'm lost.

Theresa (*to Dora*) His mother is always with him.

Dora Yes, I got that, dear, thanks very much.

Ruth (*to Young Thomas*) *Schläfst du?* [Are you asleep?]

Young Thomas *Scho.* [Yes.]

Ruth *Aber du bist auch wach?* [But are you also awake?]

Dora laughs.

Young Thomas *Na.* [No.]

Dora laughs. Thomas laughs.

Ruth *Ich habe doch gesagt, wenn du stark bist, habe ich ein Geschenk für dich.*

Dora *Stark?*

Theresa If he is strong, she has something for him.

Dora What kind of something?

Young Thomas *Wos iss n?*

Dora That's what *I* want to know.

Ruth (*putting nothing in his hand*) *Augen zu, Hand auf, jetzt fest zumachen.* [Shut your eyes, open your hand, now close tightly.]

Young Thomas *Do is nixn.* [There's nothing.]

Ruth *Versuch's nochmal. Jetzt, kannst du es fühlen?* [Try again. Now can you feel it?]

Young Thomas *Jo.* [Yes.]

Ruth *Was ist es?* [What is it?]

Young Thomas (*upset*) *I woas ned, wos des is.* [I don't know what it is.]

Ruth It's a nugget. *Ein Nugget.*

Dora A what?

Ruth *Es ist ein kleines Stück Gold.* [It's a little bit of gold.]

Young Thomas *Koa Scheiß? Des is a Goid?* [Is it really gold?]

Ruth *Nein, aber es ist wertvoll für mich.*

Theresa It's not actually gold but it's precious to her.

Young Thomas *Iss äppa dei Säi?*

Thomas (*to Ruth*) Is it your soul?

Woman (*bursting into the room*) They are here!

Banging on a door.

Dora Not in the middle of the night!

Theresa Who is it?

Dora Damn them to hell!

Ruth Thomas!

Ruth protects Young Thomas throughout.

Dora Where are my boots?

Russians sing in the street.

Ruth Don't put on the light!

Dora (*turning on the light*) Then how can I find my boots?

Ruth Now they can see us through the windows!

Dora turns out the light.

(*To Theresa*) Don't go down!

Theresa I want to know who it is!

She goes.
Doors bang open and shut.

Dora What can you see?

Ruth Soviet.

Dora Dear God. Military?

Ruth Black caps! Oh, now trucks!

Dora How many?

Ruth At the end of the street four, five.

Theresa (*coming back*) They've found out about the train!

Woman They're revving up a truck to smash down the gate!

Ruth (*to Dora*) The Polish children going on the train, get them out the back, do it now!

Dora goes. Soviet liaison officers come in.

(*To Soviet officers.*) What the devil are you doing here?

Soviet Liaison Officer You inform us all your children are Polish. Paperwork!

Olga (*arriving*) Doctor Polunina, hello. Go *there*, *all* of you! Ah, light in my eyes, aim torches at the floor!

Ruth (*to Dora*) Yes?

Dora (*to Ruth*) All good.

George (*arriving*) Polunina!

Olga My good friends –

George In the US sector –

Olga Before one hour is out –

George You are without authority!

Olga (*of Ruth*) But who gives *her* authority? No, we examine all children and organise everything. We know very well a train has been authorised to carry children to a far distant country.

Ruth A train?

Dora Going where?

Theresa We know nothing about a train.

Ruth Authorised by who?

Olga Show documentation all children going on train are Poles. If not, my duty is care for them as citizens of Soviet Russia where they will live happy as minks in their own skins.

Ruth There is no train!

Soviet Soldier (*running up*) They have now fully prepared the engine!

Olga (*to Ruth*) Do you see? I have men in every part of the station.

Soviet Soldier With hammers – ting! – they check connections between coaches.

Theresa gives a file to Ruth who gives it to Olga.

Olga This is documentation? So you say. How many? (*Reading.*) 'Katarzyna, Agnieszka, Casimir . . .' Maybe.

Olga gives the file to Ruth who gives it back to Theresa.

All the rest, children, food, beds, the whole operation is now transferred to Soviet zone!

George (*to Ruth*) Legally they can act as they like with their own people.

Russians singing.

Children *Dokąd nas zabierają? Nie chcemy iść! Boimy się. Zostawcie mnie!* [Where are they taking us? We don't want to go! We're frightened. Leave me!]

Olga They are all Vanya, they are all Natasha! Because why? Because I say so!

Children *Zostaw mnie! Chcę zostać! Nie chcę iść!* [Leave me! I want to stay! I don't want to go!]

Olga (*to Young Thomas*) *Poydem so mnoy. Ne boisys, malen'kiy tovarishch.* [Come with me. Don't be afraid, little comrade.]

George (*quietly*) Go on, Tommy boy . . .

Olga (*to Ruth*) You know who he is? Or you don't know? (*To Young Thomas.*) *Ya obeshchayu, chto nikto tebya ne obidit.* [I promise no one will hurt you.]

Young Thomas (*taking Ruth's hand, to Olga*) Des is mei Mama. [She is my mother.]

Olga Huh?

Ruth (*to Olga*) She is my mother.

Thomas Of this I remember nothing except your hand, how strong it is.

Russians (*singing*)
Arise our land
So vast and free
Sweep the foe
From the plains
For freedom strike a blow

The Soviet officers, Olga and George have gone. Ruth is still holding on to Young Thomas.

Ruth Check all the rooms.

Theresa So many climbed out the windows.

Dora They smashed the windows.

George We'll find them! We'll bring them back!

Theresa How many did they take?

Dora Impossible to know, they'll be hiding in trees, in ditches.

George We'll round them up, they won't have gone far.

Ruth (*to George*) George, I beg you . . .

George What now?

Ruth Delay the train.

Dora You want what?

Theresa (*to Ruth*) Our train leaves tomorrow at first light.

Ruth (*to Dora*) You, find somewhere safe for the Polish children.

George The Soviets will be back. Nowhere is safe.

Ruth (*to George*) It's the American zone! Where are your men? You cannot allow these brutes to get away with it!

Dora (*to Ruth*) See sense, listen to me!

Theresa (*to George*) We have to get the children across the border!

George (*to Ruth*) How long do you need?

Ruth Two days.

George It's not possible.

Dora Or wise.

Ruth (*raging, to Dora*) Is it too much for once I'm allowed to do what *I* feel is the right thing?

Dora You'll put everything we've done at risk? Just tell me the reason.

ELISE'S HOUSE 1945

Young Thomas has no idea why he is there. Ruth tries on a coat.

Elise But where to?

Ruth Here and there.

Elise For how long?

Ruth Hardly any time.

Elise That has no lining, you'll freeze, take the one with the fur collar, bad idea, the train will be filthy. Your plan is to leave him with me?

Ruth Not at all, with a friend, a photographer. Where's my bag?

Elise But surely that's why you brought him? I could do with cheerful company.

Ruth (*showing a photograph*) He took this.

Elise Oh, he's talented, he's made you look delightful.

Ruth Keep it, if you like.

Elise (*singing and dancing with her*) 'Quand il me prend dans ses bras . . .'

Ruth Oh don't. Give it back.

Elise *La la la, la la la* . . . Don't glare at me with your lion's face. (*Of Young Thomas.*) *Parle-t-il français?*

Ruth *Pas du tout.* Speak. Look, if you must know . . .

Elise Where's he disappeared to? Oh my God. Marguerite!

Ruth Calm down, he'll be in the garden, with children you must never fuss.

Elise Really? How do you know so much about it?

Ruth The day after tomorrow, listen, our plan is we'll take a group whose identities we know home, do you see, to Lubelskie province –

Elise Which is where precisely?

Ruth Imagine it, their mothers and fathers will gather from miles around to receive them.

Thomas (*to Ruth*) I should have been on the train.

Ruth About that little chap we've discovered nothing except that he's Polish so he stays.

Thomas (*to Ruth*) I should have been on the train!

Elise My child, sit with me.

Ruth Why?

Elise I want you to listen.

Ruth Speak.

Elise Russians with Russians, Poles with Poles. How is this different?

Ruth From?

Elise What *they* did.

Ruth Oh!

Elise The sacred bloodline.

Ruth *Ma mère!*

Elise 'Only Germans good enough for Germans.'

Ruth But surely, no, even you . . .

Elise What about me, in that tone of voice?

Ruth Surely, a mother's longing for her own child . . . It has nothing to do with nationality or culture. *One's very own child* . . . I must go, it takes a whole day to get back. Will you look after him?

Elise (*after a moment*) My boy, you never met me before in your life but would you like to stay in my house a few days? Yes? How would I entertain you? I know, the piano, come. This old girl is a Bösendorfer, very precious, it belonged to *maman, my maman*.

She leads him to the piano.

Try not to scratch her too badly with your shoes. Give me your finger, thank you, now one note at a time.

Elise plays a few notes. Young Thomas bangs the keys. Elise looks at Ruth. After a moment Ruth bangs the keys.

Really . . . ?

Thomas bangs the keys. Ruth bangs the keys. Thomas bangs the keys. Elise looks at Ruth, then bangs a chord. Thomas sits and plays a chord. Elise plays a little tune. Thomas plays his own little tune.

You see? What did I say? He's musical, in my opinion. Hold your hands like so. That's it. Shift up, Thomas. Good, let your fingers hang down, do you see, like sausages. Don't wriggle . . .

Ruth watches as Young Thomas and Elise play a tune . . .

(*To Ruth.*) But he *will* go back? He won't become your responsibility?

Young Thomas plays the tune . . . As Ruth goes, she takes the coat with the fur collar.

THE TRAIN 1945 – DAY

Bill takes photographs . . .

Dora (*to Bill*) Where's Ruth?

Bill (*to Dora*) On the platform checking the manifest.

Children *Nie chcę być w tym cholernym wagonie, chcę być z przodu z woźnicą.* [I don't want to be in this shitty carriage, I want to be at the front with the driver.]

Theresa (*simultaneous*) You *cannot* be with the driver, go to where I told you, all of you!

Dora All of you! (*To Theresa.*) Wood for the stoves, look, supplies for just a few days.

Bill We'll only be gone a few days.

Theresa (*counting children*) Six, eleven . . .

Children *Nie mogę patrzeć przez okno. Widzę wszystko! Chodźmy, ruszajmy!* [I can't see out the window. I can see everything! Let's go, let's move!]

Ruth is now on the train.

Theresa Fourteen, eighteen, twenty-one, twenty-four! Ruth, every child accounted for.

Dora (*to Ruth*) So, you did it?

Dora, Theresa and Bill look at Ruth.

Ruth I did.

Thomas (*to Ruth*) You left me with your mother because you'd no idea what to do with me.

Dora (*to Ruth*) Can't natter, too much to do.

Ruth (*to Thomas*) I always have an idea, it's my nature. (*To Dora.*) Are you coming or not?

Dora Poland? Why would I want to? It's just I can't bear to say goodbye to any of them.

Train whistles.

Ruth (*to Dora*) Last chance, it's now or never. (*To Thomas.*) If you'd care to read it carefully, it's in the memoir.

Dora (*to Ruth*) I don't want to go but I can't leave you.

Thomas (*to Ruth*) I'm nowhere in your memoir!

Ruth (*to Thomas*) Every word is about you.

Dora Oh, sod it.

She gets on the train and hugs Ruth.
Train whistles.

Bill Ladies, this way.

He photographs Ruth and Dora.

Children *Ruszamy się, ruszamy się!* [We're moving, we're moving!]

Theresa Sit down, sit down! Hold on for dear life!

Dora There's nothing like enough beds, not nearly.

American Soldier Hey, hey listen up. Ladies, this is Captain Mrozek, any difficulty at the border, he'll see you through.

Polish Officer *Cała przyjemność po mojej stronie!* My absolute pleasure.

Dora Ruth!

Ruth (*to children*) Sit down! (*To Dora.*) What?

Theresa Ruth, over here!

Bill (*to Ruth*) Hey, come sit here, sweets!

Ruth I can't take care of everyone all the time! Bill . . . ?

THE TRAIN 1945 – NIGHT

American Soldier As of this moment, the line's clear.

Polish Officer Cleared for you, my good friends.

Theresa (*to children*) Hold on to the seats!

Ruth (*to children*) We'll stop lurching when we reach the bottom of the valley. Sit! You too, Bill. Lola, not on the floor, it's mucky.

Theresa Excuse me, I bloody swept it.

Polish Officer A million thanks for what you are doing for our holy nation.

Dora Draw the curtains, mountains make me dizzy.

Polish Officer We travel with God.

They sleep.

Dora I've had no rest for blooming hours!

Theresa Sit down, Dora.

Dora (*raging*) Are you telling me what to do?

The train judders as it slows. Whistles. The train stops. Doors bang.

Polish Officer Border. So-called border.

Soviet Officer Papers!

Dora What now?

Polish Officer Absolute calm, ladies, do you agree? Absolute calm.

Soviet Officer Papers! I need to see papers!

Ruth (*to the Soviet Officer*) Every one of these children is Polish.

Polish Officer (*to Ruth*) If temperatures rise, you risk everything.

Ruth (*to the Soviet Officer*) Everyone's papers are in order. Let us through.

The Polish Officer speaks to the Soviet Officer. She stares at Ruth and goes.

(*To Polish Officer.*) Thank you.

Polish Officer Absolute pleasure, ladies, absolute pleasure.

Children *Ruszamy się, ruszamy się!* [We're moving, we're moving!]

THE TRAIN 1945 – DAY

Bill Ruth? Where are you? There you are. We're here.

Ruth Dora! Theresa! We're here! Everyone! We're here!

A STATION PLATFORM, CENTRAL POLAND 1945

A Polish song of welcome. Bill takes photographs.

Village Mayor But we waited on platform three days, many arrivals, nobody.

Ruth We're here now.

Village Mayor Only twenty-four, why so few?

Priest Holy Mary, Queen of Poland . . .

Congregation Pray for us.

Priest Jesus, our saviour . . .

Congregation Pray for us.

Village Mayor (*to Ruth*) And you are?

Ruth This is Lola Krawczyk.

Village Mayor My dear Lola, I am mayor of your village, we are two hundred and six with a lake to fish, a stream to swim and a world-famous view of the hills. Your mother, a beautiful soul, never ceased her search for you, when she died she suffered no pain, at her grave we planted the blue flowers she loved. Kiss your father, let him bear you up in his arms, then kiss the whole village, each woman is your mother, all of us love you, we all do.

Music. Dancing.

RUTH'S FLAT 1990

Thomas (*to Ruth*) It was at the end of the recital, New York, the Alice Tully Hall. I played the last notes.

He plays.

The floor of the auditorium is flat, he made his way through the chairs holding up his hand, like so. Why's he in such a hurry? What *is* this? Before my recital, a *trattoria* booked by the management, confusion in the kitchen, my food came late, I'd eaten no more than a mouthful, had I played so badly, was he disappointed, even angry? But his face was alight. Good God, he's climbing onto the stage. Hello, I'm Thomas Hertzveld.

Pawel (*to Thomas*) I'm taking a terrible chance, believe me, I'm shaking like a leaf.

Thomas (*to Ruth*) In some ways, it struck me even then, we look alike, the setting of the eyes, the way the hair falls . . .

Pawel (*to Thomas*) From your first notes I was transported, tears down my cheeks, am I going nuts? This is the way *I* play.

Thomas (*to Ruth*) They had moved to America in the 1980s, the Hudson Valley, they don't often come into town, my brother Pawel, my sisters, Ewa, Małgorzata. They're all musicians, my whole Polish family, all finer, more musical, than I am. I'm not modest, I'm aware of my quality but when *I* play I sweat, my audience feels what it costs me, they have *sprezzatura*, nonchalance.

Pawel (*weeping*) Janusz!

Ewa *and* **Małgorzata** Janusz.

Thomas (*to Ruth*) They inform me my name is Janusz. It should've been the highpoint of my life but darkness flowed through me. You, always you. If you'd taken *me* on the train . . .

Ruth Be fair. It's a vast country, we had no idea what part you came from.

Thomas If I'd been anywhere in my country, they might have found me!

Ruth This is overwhelming. When was this recital?

Thomas Last Friday.

Ruth *Last Friday?* And that's why you came bounding up the stairs to declare war on poor Ruth? Am *I* the enemy?

Thomas (*to Ruth*) Our father –

Pawel Died in '75 before we came to America.

Thomas (*to Ruth*) Until his heart stopped he *never* gave up looking for me.

Ewa Our mother Agnieszka drew portraits of you out of her memory.

Małgorzata She hung them on the wall.

Thomas (*to Ruth*) Or . . . if I'd stayed in the big city, London, Washington, with you . . . You buried me in the dark valley, what chance they could ever find me?

A burst of the Shostakovich Piano Quintet in G with all the instruments.

Yesterday in Brooklyn –

Ruth *Yesterday?*

Thomas They played to welcome me. The room broke open, there were no walls, no ceiling. I saw by a light as bright as day the other life, how mine might have been.

The music ends.

Ruth What can I offer you? Don't say nothing. Somewhere we have quite a good espresso machine. (*After a moment.*) In my experience, history always has one more trick up its sleeve. On the train back from Poland . . . We arrive at the station near the schloss, dawn, Bill lifts me down and for the first time – odd what one remembers – I'm in his arms. Bill. We strolled down country lanes, up the avenue of cedars to the Countess's castle . . .

THE SCHLOSS 1945

Bill Why've you stopped?

Ruth Wait.

Bill Ruth?

Ruth No, listen!

Bill I don't hear nothing.

Ruth What's going on?

Bill Meaning?

Ruth Only look in the fields! Nothing's moving!

Bill Yeah, peaceful, I'm enjoying it.

Ruth Even the horses are missing.

George Ruth, hey!

Ruth George!

George Can you see me over here waving?

Ruth (*calling*) Where are the children?

George Wait over there, folks, we'll come to you.

George comes on, followed by American soldiers carrying toys and other things left behind by the children.

Where are who?

The American soldiers laugh.

Ruth My Russians, my Ukrainians . . .

George Oh, but surely . . . *Yours?* Honey, you knew the plan.

Ruth (*to Bill*) Do you know what he's talking about?

George It was a moment none of us will forget.

Bill (*to Ruth*) I was with you.

George History.

Bill (*to Ruth*) I know nothing.

George At this moment those kids are heading to Frankfurt, then out of this hell-hole known as Europe to some of the finest homes anywhere on the planet. Minnesota.

American Soldier 1 Yes, sir!

George They'll get a pa, a ma, they'll be sucking on a tit spouting maple syrup just how it says in the holy scriptures.

American Soldier 2 Amen!

Ruth But was it what they *wanted*? George? Was it? Was it what *they* wanted? (*To Thomas.*) Working out of Passau, overnight we got the backing of every one of the UNRRA field workers, we circulated a most powerfully written protest, it's not too late, we'll get them back, I made hundreds of phone calls to congressmen in Washington, senior members of parliament in London – 'this is a gross dereliction of moral responsibility'.

George (*to Ruth*) State Department diktat – displaced kids, US long-term strategic interests, Minnesota, ba boom. (*To a soldier.*) Show her the cables.

Ruth (*to Thomas*) Even now when it comes back it's a knife gouging into, not my heart, my most deeply held conviction: good will triumph over evil. (*To George.*) *To steal children!*

George (*to Ruth*) We won the war, honey, the whole world wants to be Yankees.

Ruth (*to Thomas*) I besieged the State Department, the Foreign Office, I wrote letter after letter. 'We have noted your opinion.' If you hadn't been with *ma mère*, you'd have been whirled away in the storm with the rest of them.

Bill (*to Ruth*) So, what do we do about the Kaiser's nephew? (*To George.*) Is there a train – who would know? – to get him direct from Alsace to Frankfurt and out of here?

Ruth Bill!

George (*to Bill*) We have trains. (*To Ruth.*) 'What *they* wanted'?

The American soldiers laugh.

The bleeding-heart brigade.

George and the American soldiers go.

Bill (*to Ruth*) Sweets, I know to you he's kinda special but you gotta give him his chance. Even for the kids now in Poland, like that. (*Snaps fingers.*) Eastern Europe's gonna be drowning in collective-hoodad what's-it-ism. I know what you've lain awake imagining but, when it comes to it, why would you take him? After all, who the hell is he?

RUTH'S FLAT 1990

Ruth (*to Thomas*) 'Take you'. That's what *they* did – Nazis, Russians, Yankees brawling like wolves over innocent children. It *had* to be the dawn of a new world. They'd splattered it with shit, I had to make it clean. So, my dear, here we are at last . . . Ruth or Susanne. It was up to you.

Thomas I was ten years old.

Ruth And I was twenty! 'Why did I take you back to your home in the valley?' Dear Janusz, I never did.

THE HILLSIDE 1945

Young Thomas has a suitcase.

Ruth (*to Thomas*) We were high on the hill overlooking Hinterwössen. (*To Young Thomas.*) Look down the valley, all the way. *Kannst du dein Haus sehen?* [Can you see your house?]

Young Thomas *Na.*

Ruth (*to Thomas*) Daffodils and snow-white daisies . . . (*To Young Thomas.*) *Siehst du es nicht?* [You can't see it?]

Young Thomas *I moanad scho.* [I don't think so.]

Ruth *Aber es ist da?* [But it is there?]

Young Thomas *Jo.* [Yes.]

Ruth *Schau mich an.* No, me – (*laughing*) look at me, darling. *Schau dir jetzt dein Haus an.* [Look at me. Now look at your house.]

Thomas (*angry*) No, this isn't right, you took me all the way to the door!

Ruth No! I didn't.

Thomas But I feel it now, your strong hand . . .

Ruth You let my hand go, you climbed down the hill, rock to rock . . .

Thomas I must have turned back.

Ruth Of course you did.

Thomas Yes. Yes, I see you high up there.

Ruth But when you reached the road and caught sight of . . .

Thomas My trees, my garden . . .

Thomas's Mother is waiting, holding an infant in her arms.
Meine Mutter . . .

Ruth You ran as though the devil was after you.

Young Thomas leaves his suitcase and runs into his mother's house.

RUTH'S FLAT 1990

At the piano Thomas starts to improvise. He segues into the tune he played with Elise – then, tentatively, into his mother's lullaby.

Ruth watches and listens. Young Thomas comes out of his mother's house, fetches his suitcase and goes back into the house.

With ever greater assurance, Thomas goes on improvising. Ruth sits with him as he returns to his mother's lullaby, now with bravura.